WHILE YOU STILL HAVE

"Every page of Joyce Rupp's beautiful book is filled with practical wisdom. By meditating on the rich life of her own mother, Rupp not only shares with us timeless and life-changing lessons, but also reminds us that holiness always makes its home in humanity, and that saints are everywhere. I loved this book!"

James Martin, S.J.
Author of *Jesus: A Pilgrimage*

"Joyce Rupp's memoir of her mother Hilda is beautiful, honest, and graced with astonishing insights into what it means to be a daughter, a mother, a human being. Her account of how this resilient woman raised eight children on an Iowa farm at first reminded me of Tim Russert's loving memoir of his father—the stories are that good. But when I got to Joyce's tender journey with her mother through the process of dying I could not help but think of C. S. Lewis's *A Grief Observed*—the book is that good. When I finished reading, I put the book down and could think of nothing other than what I had just read. *Fly While You Still Have Wings* is Joyce Rupp's best book ever, a total original, and I would not be surprised if it became a classic."

Michael Leach
Author of *Why Stay Catholic?*

"This beautiful memoir of her mother displays the remarkable gifts that have earned Joyce Rupp so many loyal readers: engaging storytelling, moving poetry, personal experiences shared with honesty and insight, and depictions of grace breaking into the most ordinary human events. In Joyce's deft telling, her mother's story becomes not only the inspiring portrait of a strong woman, but also a primer on the mother-daughter relationship and the meaning of love and limits, suffering and courage, grief and healing. Her book's most important contribution may be the wisdom she offers on how to meet the challenges and discover the blessings of giving and receiving care in life's later years."

Kathleen Fischer
Author of *Winter Grace: Spirituality and Aging*

"Joyce Rupp's best book yet. How many of us would like to pay tribute to our mothers by acknowledging the lessons learned from them that still guide us, and reflect on what we wished we had done in her later years and failed to do, or what we did do and wished we had not? Joyce does this beautifully and becomes our teacher in this honest memoir."

Trish Herbert
Author of *Journeywell: A Guide to Quality Aging*

WHILE YOU STILL HAVE

AND OTHER LESSONS MY
RESILIENT MOTHER TAUGHT ME

JOYCE RUPP

SORIN BOOKS Notre Dame, Indiana

Excerpt from the poem "Riverflow" from *Riverflow: New & Selected Poems* by David Whyte, copyright © 2012 by David Whyte. Used with permission of the author and Many Rivers Press (www.davidwhyte.com).

"If You Have Nothing" by Jessica Powers from *The Selected Poetry of Jessica Powers* edited by R. Siegfried and Robert Morneau, copyright 1989, 1999 by Carmelite Monastery, Pewaukee, WI. Used with permission.

---

www.sorinbooks.com

Paperback: ISBN-13 978-1-933495-84-2

E-book: ISBN-13 978-1-933495-85-9

Cover image © Thinkstock.com.

Cover and text design by Brian C. Conley.

Printed and bound in the United States of America.

Library of Congress Cataloging-in-Publication Data is available.

TO MY BELOVED MOTHER

HILDEGARD CECELIA ANTOINETTE WILBERDING

MARCH 24, 1916–APRIL 20, 2000

CONTENTS

ACKNOWLEDGMENTS

Whenever I complete a manuscript and send it off to the publishing company, I do so with a keen awareness that many people have helped to bring the book to birth. This is certainly true for *Fly While You Still Have Wings*: so many have directly or indirectly touched its pages with the gift of their insights, critiques, information, supportive prayer, and presence.

Pieces of my mother's history were lost to me until I found them through my siblings and other relatives who generously shared their stories. My older sister Lois Chettinger, who lived near our mother and provided immense help and consolation to Mom as she aged, filled in many of the missing pieces in the manuscript with her treasured remembrances. She offered valuable suggestions and endless encouragement. My older brother Jerry Rupp and his wife, Melanie, were also a source of memories and continually cheered me on. One of my younger sisters, Jeanne Somsky, provided the genealogy details.

Mom's sister Della Broderson and her two first cousins Dorothy Schnoes and Kitty Kohn gifted me with their experiences and recollections of my mother's early family life in Remsen, Iowa. My cousin Robert Sanders had no idea how much his words would influence my work on this memoir. His note came when I languished in doubt about how to proceed: "I think that memoir will be an amazing new reflection on living and dying. And not only a great-to-come addition to your body of work, but probably a healing and intimate experience for you to write." I kept that note next to my computer for an entire year. It helped me turn a significant corner in my willingness to complete the memoir and stay on course.

Close friends and authors assisted with valuable writing helps. How much I learned from Mary Kay Shanley, who teaches memoir, as I listened to her presentations when we co-led writing retreats for women. Macrina Wiederkehr listened patiently as I read chapters of the manuscript to her. Trish Herbert shared the wisdom she gleaned from writing and teaching about the journey of aging. Trish, along with Robin Kline, helped immensely with honest critiques of my first draft.

Two friends from Toronto, Canada—John Pollard, presenter of workshops on *Mindful Living and Conscious Dying*, and Austin Repath, who writes with vulnerable insight regarding his own movement into the later years of life—influenced my resolve to trust the healing aspect of writing the memoir.

Then there are those amazingly kind persons whose hospitality of a quiet place for solitude and beauty allowed me the opportunity to "hide out" and delve deeply into the writing process: Katie Bloom, Tim and Trudy Barry, Mike and Mary Mahoney, and Bill Walker. Likewise, I am greatly indebted to Beth Waterhouse, director of the *Ernest Oberholtzer Foundation* on Mallard Island in Rainy Lake, Minnesota. One of my most profound moments in writing this book took place during the time I spent there.

While I was absorbed in working with the manuscript, Faye Williamson managed my website with attentive care, as she always does. Janet Barnes and Frieda Molinelli continued to support my life and ministry with the treasured gift of their daily prayer. The members of the weekly reflection group to which I belong kept my heart humming with hope: Rebecca Kemble, Shelley Erickson, Mary Ferring, Joyce Hutchison, Mary Jones, Mary Mahoney, Kathy Quinn, Kathy Reardon, and Kathi Sircy.

I learned a lot about aging from members of my Servite community as I observed how they approach their entrance into elderhood. I'm grateful for their kind support along with all those persons older than I am who inspire me with their ability to "fly while they still have wings."

My greatest thanks go to my faithful and skilled editor, Robert Hamma. His kind manner, wise suggestions, and constant enthusiasm for this book provided me with what I required to hone and craft it into a final version that we both could applaud. I am also conscious of how much the staff in each department at Ave Maria Press supports my published work. In particular, I wish to thank Kristen Hornyak Bonelli and Brian Conley for their sensitive and magical ability to create a cover for this book that truly expresses what lies within it.

To all who sent affirming messages regarding my written work during the time of writing this memoir the past five years, I give a huge thank you. Those statements of belief in my ability to write in a way that speaks to readers' lived experience assured me that I could do so within the pages of this book. Thank you, dear readers, for your valuable support.

PREFACE

The Burial

We carried her out then
with the strong chorus of farm folk
resounding "How Great Thou Art,"
carried her from the little country church
where she prayed and served
for forty-nine years,
where she fried chicken and baked pies
for parish dinners, sewed garments for the poor,
cleaned pews, washed linens
and made Jell-O salads for funeral dinners.
The burial entourage walked behind her,
passed a lonely, vacant building
that schooled her eight children,
where she stood up to nuns who went
beyond the boundaries of discipline
and bore the scalding words
of an alcoholic pastor's false judgments,
yet remained strong and stalwart in a faith

that might easily have crumbled for others
in similar circumstance.

Onward we walked to the cemetery
where a considerable number of tombstones
bore her husband's last name but not one
of her own ancestry. We stood
silently at the gravesite, each mourner's sorrow
bearing the certainty of her death. As the
pastor uttered the last prayer a lone bird,
a robin perhaps, warbled a sparkling song
of commencement. (Did it sing for you, my mother?
And was the soft, gentle breeze sweeping
across our faces a final farewell from you?)

I lifted my eyes beyond the flower-laden casket
to the freshly planted fields beyond,
looked across the flat mile or so to the tall evergreens
marking the front lawn of the family farm.
In that brief moment I glimpsed
the wholeness of life's quickly erased journey,
and marveled at its simplicity.

—Joyce Rupp

A resilient life is not an impenetrable fortress.
A resilient life is more like a calm, deep river
that soothes the suffering soul within us and in those
around us.

—James Kullander
Mastering the Art of Resilience

Ever since my mother, Hilda Rupp, died fourteen years ago I have wanted to write this book. The way she lived, aged, and approached her death taught me how I hope to engage with my own. So why has it taken me this long to gather the memories and insights I've gleaned from her life? Why have I started and stopped so often in these years long since passed?

Each time I recalled my mother's presence, tears flowed. I thought, "I'll wait to write about her until the sadness is out of my system." However, the sadness did not leave. I finally took a deep breath and pushed myself into the writing process. Without realizing it, each page I wrote moved me further into my healing.

Is the sorrow gone now? Not completely. I realize I will always miss my mother's presence. She was too dear for me to not retain a certain sense of loss. I have come to accept this.

As I gradually came to know my mother, not only as an aging parent but as a friend, I grew in admiration of her resiliency. Time and again, I recognized how she did not allow ongoing hardships and difficult deaths to dampen her zestful and generous spirit. I ought not to have been surprised at this once I looked into the etymology of her name and discovered that "Hildegard" comes from a Scandinavian myth in which Hildegard is a maiden who escorts those in battle.

True to her name's origin, my mother lived alongside some challenging "battles" in her lifetime and managed them with courage. She brought this resiliency of her younger years into elderhood and most of the time it prevailed. Even though I felt sadness about Mom's increasing frailty, I could not comprehend very well the devastating effect of this emerging diminishment. After Mom's death, when I thought about the last years of her life, I felt a haunting distress about what I wished I had done and failed to do, and what I *did* do and wished I had not.

A good portion of my tears came from the absence that death brings and from a continual surge of misgivings. How I longed to have been more aware of the inside story of letting go that comes creeping in with the limitations of aging. It has taken me these many years to finally leave those regrets behind and intentionally move on from them.

While I extol my mother's style of aging and dying, I do not wish to present her as a saint. Hilda Rupp had her quirks and faults, as we all do. They did not, however, prevent her from being admired and appreciated by relatives, friends, and acquaintances.

Nor does the example of how my mother lived and aged deny the experience of countless older persons whose health of body, mind, and spirit differs significantly from her situation and circumstance. Not every aging person can approach life and death as my mother did. Plenty of physical health problems plagued Mom in the fourteen years before death, but her mind was relatively steady and alert until the end. Countless elderly persons do not have this option due to cognitive issues, such as those associated with dementia and Alzheimer's disease.

Yet it is my hope that what I learned from my mother in her aging and dying process will benefit others, both those entering their later years and those who accompany or care for them. I trust this book will assist those who maintain a relationship with an aging individual not to repeat the regrettable mistakes that ensued from my inability to understand what it is like to "grow old."

I also hope this book will help those in their elderhood find renewed confidence. Perhaps my mother's attitude will lend credence to the belief that the lessening of good health and vitality can be met with a positive approach, one that does not deny the angst of this loss, but also allows for the joy and satisfaction in what is yet possible.

This is not a "rah-rah, cheerleader-for-the-elderly" book. There are enough of those around, suggesting older people must continue to look and act twenty years younger than they are. This type of literature exacerbates the Western world's idolization of youth and lessens the value of leaning into the aging process with dignity and the gutsy honesty that accepts the situation of aging for what it is.

I most wish to convey the inspiration I received from the way my mother met her elder years. She gave me courage to meet my own. This is not to say my aging process is going to be any easier. Rather, when I recall my mother's approach to life and death I believe that I, too, can maintain a positive outlook. I can learn to live with and accept my physical decline and the limitations accruing with it in a way that contributes positively to my own personal transformation and to the benefit of those companioning me in my senior years.

None of us knows how our final stage of life will affect us until we experience it. We do know that we want to live life with as much quality and verve as possible, for as long as we can. My mother's motto in her last decade was "Fly while you still have wings." She intentionally lived with enthusiasm and gratitude. Then there came a time when those strong wings were not so sturdy anymore. She initially met this reality with fierce resistance. Eventually, she leaned into what could not be changed, doing so with the wisdom of one who believes old age and death can be met with a faith-filled acceptance and confident serenity.

This I learned from my resilient mother.

INTRODUCTION

Sorrow

Memories endure
of a glass-paned door,
the veined hand
behind it
waving
a tender farewell,
the gray smile
pretending to be brave
imprinting itself
on my mind
with permanent ink.

Will this sadness
over my mother's death
never leave?
Will sorrow huddle
in the strong shell
of determined grief
and fix its claim
on my heart
until I, too, depart?

Perhaps.
Perhaps not.

Maybe now,
after these many years,
I can curve
my love with ease
toward sorrow,
until peace
rests like a child
in her mother's arms.

Perhaps I can learn
to receive sorrow
like an old friend
who simply asks
not to be forgotten.

—**Joyce Rupp**

Those who will not slip beneath
    the still surface on the well of grief,
turning down through its black water
    to the place we cannot breathe,
will never know the source from which we drink,
    the secret water, cold and clear. . . .

—David Whyte
River Flow

An urge to be by water kept stirring as I began writing about my mother. I followed that yearning one day and went for a walk by Saylorville Lake. I chose a perfect day, although I did not know this until I sat by the water's edge on a late afternoon. Perfect because the wind had picked up speed all day and tossed lake water onto the sandy shore with a sound reminiscent of the sea. I closed my eyes and listened to the spirited waters. Slowly I heard something more—the slosh and swish of being in the womb of Hildegard Cecelia Antoinette Wilberding. Then I knew the puzzling yearning to be by water was calling me to honor and remember the intimate relationship with my mother, a bond begun when I dwelt in her watery womb.

In spite of being pregnant, my mother worked long, strenuous days as a farm wife. Already having birthed two young children under the age of five, I doubt she allowed herself to sit down and rest for any significant amount of time. During gestation my tiny, evolving body must have felt a steady movement similar to those energetic waves of lake water moving back and forth.

Thinking about this rhythm of wombed oneness moved me deeply, eliciting unexpected emotion. I marveled, "Here I am today, sixty-eight years of life, the result of my mother's fertilized egg taking root in the precious cavity of her uterus." Out of this profound truth a tremendous gratitude arose for the life I received from her.

I had a loving relationship with my mother. Some do not. But no matter—we are all influenced by our time in the womb. For it is there we find the life that initially shapes and forms us into who we are. Whether we are conscious of it or not, when a mother dies a part of us dies too. The umbilical cord of connection might have been severed at our birth, but there remains an invisible link between a mother and the one she brought to life. We cannot have fed and grown inside her without having this experience firmly embedded in our psyche.

Musings about my birth were not the end of water's ability to lead me to unexpected insights about my maternal relationship. After that initial experience with water, I set aside further writing due to the daily push of endless deadlines. Six months later I paused for a week of writing at Lake Okoboji where I refocused on my mother by combing through more of my daily journals for memories. There, by the waters of this deep glacial lake, I came across an entry in which Mom described my birth: "With you I had lots of water when it broke, more than with any of the other ones."

No wonder my deeper self kept insisting "water, water."

Four weeks after Lake Okoboji, I resumed writing when I arrived at Mallard Island in Rainy Lake for a writer's residency program. I had not given much thought as to where I would be, other than knowing Mallard Island was situated close to the wildness of Minnesota's northern boundary waters, away from both internet and phone service. Much to my surprise and delight the coordinator assigned me to Cedarbark Cabin, where my bed rested in an alcove extending over the water. As I went to bed that first evening, lullabied to sleep with the lake's gentle lapping sounds, I wondered what new treasures water held for me.

The next morning I left the cabin at dawn and strolled to the end of the small island. There I crossed a narrow stone bridge and walked up to what would become a sanctuary of healing. Before me stood the Japanese House, named most probably for its structural simplicity and openness. Built in a little square with walls of local wood and light-filled windows opening to nature's beauty, it rests over a promontory of stones and lake water.

As I sat there at the small wooden table provided for artists and writers, the tranquility of the place allowed a strong sorrow to surface. Tears trickled as I thought of the many deceased I loved, particularly my mother. How much I missed her still, more than eleven years after her death. I realized, too, I still had not let go of my regrets—those things I wished I had done more of to ease her last years of aging and dying. I wondered to myself that morning, "Will

I ever be free from this angst that perpetually rises up in me?"

I left the Japanese House that morning with this question still unresolved. All day it hung around nagging insistently for a response while I tried to write about the woman whose life held valuable teachings for me. On the second morning, after another night of sleeping above the water, I again went to my sanctuary of healing. This time, without realizing what I was doing (for so it is when intuition rises and the rational becomes stilled), I sat down on the slender doorsill in front of the table so I could face out to the water and the neighboring islands.

All of a sudden I thought, "Oh! I am sitting on the doorsill, the threshold, the place of being neither in nor out, the place of 'don't know.'" I smiled, recognizing how I was led to sit on a spot symbolic of my internal space. Somehow that unplanned move to the threshold freed me to "be." So pronounced was the harmony and peacefulness of the little house that I easily let the question of what to do with my grief-filled regrets and sense of loss slip away.

I felt the spirit of the place and the lake water embrace me. I had no desire for either a helpful insight or a change of emotion. I just sat in that serene spot over the water, sat on the threshold and waited. For what I did not know.

Sometime during those two hours at the Japanese House, the inner gate opened. As I gazed at the idyllic scene before me, the myth of the river Styx pierced my subdued consciousness like an Olympic diver hitting the water. I remembered the tale of how Greeks placed their dead on boats so the river Styx could carry them to the other side of this life. Water, bearing the dead. Water, conveying them away in honor. Water, moving them onward with hope of something beyond. Water, comforting those left behind.

Instantly I found clarity regarding my regrets and sadness. I was to let go of the aspects of my mother's death that held me captive. I could place all this upon the water and let it, too, travel onward. I was to focus on my mother's life, to embrace her love, and to surrender my loss. I had done what I could. It was enough.

The sloshing waters of Saylorville Lake led me to remember life in my mother's womb. Rainy Lake led me to accept her death, an entrance into the Eternal Womb. Although I remained behind, I was not bereft and orphaned anymore. Instead, bountiful memories remained to be cherished for the rest of my life.

At that moment of acceptance, I entered into the full circle of life-death-rebirth. There by the northern waters I knew why I was to come to a small island where land barely has a voice compared to the vast speech of water. I understood why each night I was to sleep on the wings of a lake and wake to its exquisite peacefulness.

It is with this peace and acceptance that I now unfold for you the story of my resilient mother's journey.

CHAPTER 1

THE BIRTH *of* RESILIENCE

The Aunts

> They came
> laden with armfuls
> of food
> and hearts overflowing
> with endless
> laughter.
>
> They came
> with a sense of well-being
> and a generous spirit,
> leaving behind
> in their own home and heart
> tribulations
> in need of caring.
>
> They came,
> these great aunts of mine,
> to steady and strengthen
> my motherless mother
> tending ten siblings
> in the Great Depression.

They came,
not for the purpose
of teaching or preaching,
but to lend a hand
in a troublesome time.

They came
with resilient spirits,
messengers of how to endure
and thrive,
to find joy
in pieces of brokenness.

They came
leaving a legacy
in the ancestral lineage,
the hope
of better times
when all seems lost.

—Joyce Rupp

> The art of resilience asks . . . that you make your
> whole life a work of art. The uncertainties of life,
> the pain and problems, let them become woven into
> the fabric of your being—alongside the joys and the
> triumphs. This is life's promise to you, not that you
> will always get what you think you want, but that you
> can become great enough to embrace it all. Live your
> life fully—there is no easier way. Make your life a
> work of art—it is enough.
>
> **—Carol Orsborn**
> *The Art of Resiliency*

No matter how young or old we are, each of us contains a story. The longer we live, the more that story includes. When I look at the history of my mother, Hilda, I see a story based on a quality of inner strength that took shape during a shattering event in her youth. Her story reminds me that resilience doesn't just happen. The seed of this attribute lodges itself at birth but remains dormant until challenging situations awaken and draw it forth.

I found an unexpected insight related to my mother's experience in Francis Weller's *Entering the Healing Ground*.[1] There I learned about "ancestral grief." "Why didn't I think of this?" I wondered, as I read his sensitive description of this type of loss. Weller refers to the "unattended pain" of the ancestors, suggesting that "the grief we carry in our bodies from sorrows experienced by (them)" can continue to linger unconsciously in us "in a layer of silence." When I came across the suggestion that we carry the grief of our ancestors deep in our psyches, it struck a strong chord of recognition. In it I heard the strains of my mother's own ancestral story.

Weller notes that the ancestors who migrated to this country did not have time to grieve the departure from their land and culture. They were forced into immediate activity and hard work, trying to settle and survive in a foreign land. People quickly gave their entire energy to going on with their lives, making an effort to survive and adjust as well as possible to their new way of existence. Consequently, they developed a "stoic facade" which did not allow for attentiveness to their loss.

This was certainly true of Cecelia Meyer Wilberding, my maternal grandmother. Although she did not suffer the direct loss of migration, she, too, had much that required her utmost attention in trying to feed and clothe eleven children. Due to the family's low income, little time and thought could be given to what stirred interiorly. The same could be said for my mother, Cecilia's daughter. Circumstances did not allow the opportunity to tend the significant loss that she experienced at the age of seventeen.

This loss happened swiftly. On the morning after her high school graduation ceremony, Mom walked to St. Mary's church for Mass and sat among her ten siblings. They dutifully participated on the first Friday of each month, having been taught that they gained special graces the Catholic Church promised for their attendance. On this particular day she sat with quiet apprehension. As the last prayer ended, a close neighbor of theirs came into the church, leaned over her and whispered, "Hilda, your mother passed this morning. So did the baby boy."

Years later when Mom recounted those devastating words, she explained why she had sensed her mother's coming death that day: "As soon as I saw our neighbor I knew what she was going to tell me. I helped clean up the pool of blood in the bedroom the night before when my mother started hemorrhaging. It was an awful sight, all that blood. As she was taken to the hospital, I looked at her white, strained face and had a feeling she was not coming home."

In the days following that heartbreaking death, the reality of becoming a surrogate mother to her ten siblings pressed Mom into immediate household responsibilities. As the oldest daughter, she assumed the task of helping her father care for the rest of the children. She had already assisted her mother with the work but now this effort advanced to full-time duty. There was work to be done, and she needed to do it. She could pay little attention to the heartache within her. My mother's sorrow went unattended.

Kitty Kohn, one of my older cousins, mentioned seeing my forty-four-year-old grandmother with the infant boy in her arms lying in the coffin. What a heart-rending scene that must have been. Mom did not speak about her mother's death very often, but when she did I noticed little emotion came forth in telling about it. It all seemed quite matter-of-fact, as if she resolutely put the past behind but wanted me to know how much it influenced her life's story. Perhaps it was her way of saying, "Look, I made it though all of that, and I'm okay."

I responded to the telling of the story quite differently. Each time I heard this weighty loss described a palpable surge of sadness and ache pushed its way into my gut, leaving me wanting to cry for the pain that Mom experienced with my grandmother's death. Although I could not name it, my mother's unattended sorrow nested inside of me. Only when I read Weller's insights into ancestral grief did I finally grasp how I had inherited that grief. From grandmother to mother to daughter it was handed down, and there I was, holding the sorrow for them.

One of the surprising gifts in writing about my mother's story of resilience is that it led to the "healing ground" of my ancestral loss. As I completed this memoir, I realized that grief over my maternal heritage no longer claims me. Entering my mother's story of life allowed the opportunity to delve into that pain and let it go. A profound gratitude now occupies the space that grief once filled.

A kind of stoicism could have hardened my mother's young spirit and left her without an ability to show care or to become absorbed in self-pity. Neither occurred. Instead, she gradually developed a quality of positive endurance that persisted throughout much of her life. My mother's resilience in her elder years was formed from the strength of character she developed during this phase of her youth. It enabled her to go forth with courage and determination when future life events threatened to snuff out hope and joy.

For many who come through adversities with strength of character, their lives may seem quite ordinary to an outsider. So it was with my mother. She bore the undistinguished characteristics of an ordinary daughter, and later, a farmwife. The extraordinary aspect of her story is how she managed to maneuver through daily hurdles with such inner dexterity. Although she experienced times of being deluged with frustration, anger, sorrow, and other unwanted emotions, beneath this rested an undying strength that surfaced repeatedly to restore confidence and peace until she took her last breath.

In reflecting on her childhood, Mom commented, "We lived during the time of the Great Depression of 1929 and were always in debt. We had so little, sometimes just bread and milk to eat. My dad only paid a part of whatever he owed. He had a huge list of bills when he died." No wonder they were unable to make the payments. Her mother gave birth every two years. Besides the son who died with her and a daughter who also succumbed in infancy, eleven children—all under the age of nineteen—survived.

In spite of their poverty and before her mother's death, Mom's parents traveled some two hundred and seventy miles across Iowa every summer, from their home in Remsen to Dyersville, to visit her maternal grandparents, Clemens and Mary Meyer. With that many children and not enough space in their old Model A Ford, the children traded off each year on which ones went along for the visit. Even so, they could only fit in the small car by the youngest children sitting on the oldest ones' laps, the others balancing on top of two small tin pails on the floor behind the front seat.

One time, when wistfully reminiscing about these trips, Mom sighed, "My mother was a saint." Then she added, "Mother was never harsh or tough on us. Dad always did the correcting and punishing. She worked extremely hard and had little time to rest. I think the only time she was really happy was when she got to visit her parents [my great-Grandpa and Grandma Meyer] in Dyersville." (The family was thrilled with what they brought home from those visits—gifts they couldn't afford to buy—such as a new iron, a comforter, or the special gift of clothes or books.)

I often wondered when Mom spoke about those trips to Dyersville how she must have longed to have her own mother alive when she was a young married woman. She never had the joy of a caring mother to be with her, to give good advice or gift her with those niceties that moms know just how to choose, no mother to help her with a newborn or pay a welcome visit. Yet, Mom never voiced this regret. She simply accepted this painful reality.

Even before her mother's death, Mom's inner strength surfaced. At graduation from St. Mary's High School she received the award of a black Schaeffer pen in recognition of a unique achievement: not missing *one day* of elementary or secondary classes. How she managed to accomplish this feat remains a marvel. At times, she must have felt miserable with a cold or flu, but she obviously let nothing stand in the way of achieving that goal. Mom was proud of her Schaeffer pen and kept it throughout her life as a quiet reminder, not only of what she achieved, but also of her stamina.

She needed that tenacity. Her dad, Joe Wilberding, whom people called "Pops," lost most of his income as a mason during the Depression when few people could afford to build anything. Eventually he found part-time employment as a city policeman and magistrate. He brought his aptitude for order and discipline home with him, insisting meals be served on time and refusing to tolerate lateness. Dishes were washed immediately following the meal. When the children argued about whose turn it was, he devised a schedule for them. After dishes at night, homework followed. This greatly helped my mother keep order in the home and taught her how to manage her own family household later on.

Emil, the eldest son, found a job at a local grocery store. The compassionate owner recognized the family's situation and regularly sent soon-to-spoil items home with Emil. Mom smiled as she recalled, "Oh, how we enjoyed special treats like the crushed pieces of candy sometimes included in the sacks Emil brought to us."

The family managed to get by with this food and the produce from their two large gardens, one near the house and another on a hill several blocks away. Along with the other children, Mom worked these gardens and carried heavy sacks of potatoes and vegetables down the street to home. Sometimes she and her sister Della biked to the big family garden. This could be a dangerous venture. "Lucky we were not killed," Mom said of the time they put the hoe across the handle bars, went speeding downhill and came too close to the concrete abutment of a bridge, hitting it head on. Fortunately, neither was hurt seriously.

Each child had a job in the gardens in addition to household tasks, with Mom leading the process of canning garden products for the winter months. The older girls joined her in this and other chores like cooking, cleaning, sewing, and mending. Mom made dresses for the girls out of all sorts of old clothing, including her dad's worn-out coveralls. They seldom owned store-bought clothes, the exception being a graduation dress of Mom's purchased by a woman whose children she watched before her mother died. This kind gesture and those of others served to instill a generosity in Mom that flowed freely throughout her life.

My mother's resiliency gained nurturance from the roots of a strong German heritage. Her maternal aunts: Ida, Olivia (Ole), Clara, Matilda (Tillie), and Jean each conveyed a remarkable ability to endure life's difficulties. Lending a hand and heart required a lot from them because each woman faced her own set of challenging circumstances. These sisters of my grandmother did all they could to help the motherless family, especially Aunt Ida and Aunt Ole. Aunt Ida had a houseful of children and a husband without a job. They lived on government food stamps even though Ida was a hard worker and cleaned houses to bring in much-needed income. Aunt Ole, who raised her children alone after her husband died from a heart attack, was equally generous with her attentiveness and care.

I never detected bitterness or defeatism in these great aunts. As a young child, I took their constant generosity and good-heartedness for granted. Quick, hearty laughter spilled out of them. In spite of the little they had, they never came empty-handed or empty-hearted, bringing food and hand-me-down clothes along with their joy. They became a natural part of our extended family. I felt such comfort in their presence. With each visit, I sensed the love they felt for my mother. A knock would be heard at the back door of our old farmhouse and one of them would come in, greeting my mother with "Hi, Hilde!" (which they pronounced "Hill-dee,"), an affectionate nickname used only by people especially close to her. They continued to offer support to my mother long into her married years. These sturdy, spirited women taught my mother by their stoutheartedness how to enter the fray of life with optimism.

As I reflect on my mother's story, I see how she developed these same features. Although she did not have an easy life, Mom was not prone to complaining. She kept at what life required with determination and the kind of faithfulness one soon takes for granted. After marriage she became like my great aunts, visiting others in need and bringing both helpful aid and comfort.

In her later years Mom insisted, "I've had a good life," and she meant it, choosing to focus on the positive and leave the not-so-good behind. She looked at her life's story without denying the difficulties, moving forward to enjoy what she could. The challenging consequences of her mother's early death and the hardships that followed engraved a robust spirit in my mother that she counted on through the rest of her life.

I don't think my mother paid much attention to her hardy response to life's challenges. She certainly did not see herself creating the "work of art" which Orsborn suggests in the excerpt at the beginning of this chapter. She just maneuvered through those ups and downs with steadfastness, counting on the durable quality of resilience to see her through whatever happened. And it did.

CHAPTER 2

FACING HARDSHIPS

Legacy of Endurance

I pause to consider
the colorful zinnias
standing firmly
in a transparent vase.

They are alive, cheerful,
a legacy of endurance.

Their survival has been
exceedingly difficult under
a piercing August sun
and early September dryness.

And I, in my heartache,
sip from their beauty,
drink in their strength,
taste their ability to stand tall

while the slow, rising promise
of release grows within me,

while I remember
my resilient mother,
also a legacy of endurance,

a paragon of how seasons
of hardship
cannot prevent a strong soul
from standing tall.

—**Joyce Rupp**

We know by now that life gives us many surprises,
that there is much we cannot control in our lives, but
that there are many different, better or worse, ways to
react to what happens.

—**Trish Herbert**
Journeywell

Where do we find the courage to maintain confidence,
to stay with what tries insistently to trample our spirit?
How do we continue to keep the flame of hope alive in a
corner of our heart when hardship strains to snuff it out?
If I were to name one book that most enabled me to meet
life's challenges it would be *Man's Search for Meaning*. In
this book Viktor Frankl records his brutal experience as
a prisoner in the death camp at Auschwitz. Through the
years I've returned often to this vivid portrayal of survival
amid appalling, inhumane conditions. While in this desolate
camp Frankl became convinced that everything can be
taken from a person, "everything but one thing: the last
of the human freedoms—to choose one's attitude in any
given set of circumstances, to choose one's own way."[1]

My mother's life held nothing comparable to Frankl's
desperate years in Auschwitz, but she did have significant
hardships and she chose how to meet them. The struggles
that came her way reflected those of others living in the
Great Depression and the following years fraught with
struggle. During those tough times most people knew
some element of poverty as they attempted to exist with
a minimum of necessities. This was true of my mother's

situation before and after she married. Only in the last two decades of her life did she manage to free herself from financial concerns.

When my mother faced hardship, she chose to rely on her inner fortitude. It proved to be one of her most worthy and necessary qualities, not only when she took on the role of mothering her younger siblings, but also when, four years later in 1937, she married my father, Lester P. Rupp. Her positive attitude made a considerable difference. She surrendered to what was required, accepted ceaseless labor as a part of farm life, and gave herself fully to it. In choosing this attitude, her resilience was strengthened rather than weakened.

As a carefree youngster I knew how hard my mother worked. What I did not know is that she recorded a lot of this in her daily diaries, which I discovered in reading them after her death. Each day Mom usually described the weather, listed some of the work she did, along with what was baked or cooked, and named anyone who came to visit. The following entries, at age forty-seven, are typical of the details included.

> Hot and humid. Did 10 loads of wash. Waxed all hardwood floors. Baked 2 cakes. Got vegetables from garden. Men combined and baled hay. [This meant she made dinner for them.] (July 24, 1965)
>
> Cleaned the house. Waxed living room floor. Baked 2 cakes. Made a lot of rolls and cinnamon

bread. Went to Rosary at VFW. Pete Ament
staying with us tonight. (September 14, 1965)

It seemed as though most everything in her life demanded
constant effort, leaving barely any time for herself. Yet, she
kept to her tasks with diligence and determination, with
the belief that she would not only survive the day-to-day
sweat and toil, but that something of value could be gleaned
because of her attentiveness to duty and demand.

Guests who visited our family met a friendly woman
of medium height and build. Hilda's fine brown hair and
warm cocoa eyes fit well with the soft face and easy smile
that welcomed them. She might initially appear a bit
nondescript, wearing little makeup, if any, and with hands
rough-skinned from scrubbing and countless other chores.
The visitors would soon be caught up in her extroverted
interest in people and the indefatigable energy that led her
to be a woman who multitasked long before it became
designated as such.

Callers at our home knew my mother had a gift for
hospitality. If they arrived unexpectedly, Mom most
probably was wearing a soiled apron when she answered
the door. After an invitation to come in, they were soon
offered a cup of coffee and some freshly baked item. Lots
of people ate at our home, and all acknowledged Hilda
Rupp's cooking to be exceptional. Mom could create
something tasty out of most anything. Little did I know
(until I went to college) that not everyone ate fried pig
brains, pickled heart, or head cheese—a gluttonous mass
created out of pig tail, tongue, and "other little pig parts."

In the wintertime, the hunger-producing aroma of oxtail soup (yes, made from the tail of a steer) met us at the door when we came home from school. When we played out in the snow, we looked forward to our special treat once back indoors: deep-fat-fried, sugar-coated bread dough.

From my youth I remember Mom engaged in what some would now term "sheer drudgery," living in a century-old farmhouse without electricity or running water. But I also remember my mother being more happy than sad. She had a way of entering into her life, as Frankl suggests, by choosing how to respond to it. In later elderhood, this attitude kept her from sagging into emotional and mental inertia. She learned in those hard years on the farm how to find within the tough stuff the place where satisfaction thrived.

Mom's brief respite from poverty occurred when she worked away from her family home, before marrying Dad. When her next-youngest sisters, the twins Armella and Della, graduated from high school, Mom decided the time was ripe to test her wings and leave Remsen to find a paying job. With her father's blessing, she found work in Cherokee, just twenty-one miles away. There she worked as a live-in nanny and housekeeper, first for the owner of a department store and later for a lawyer's family. She transitioned to a very different situation: away from poverty to a comfortable life, away from the responsibility of many children to a few, away from a crowded house to a spacious home. No wonder Mom's eyes lit up whenever she talked about that brief chapter in her history.

Marriage bumped her back into poverty. *The Remsen Bell* describes my parent's marriage in glowing detail, the wedding Mass taking place at the ungodly hour of 8:30 a.m. The wedding photo reveals a handsome man with curly, black hair standing next to a pretty bride with a Dove-soap complexion. The paper reads: "Immediately after the ceremony, breakfast was served at the home of the bride's father, with Miss Della Wilberding, the bride's sister, as hostess. At high noon a two-course dinner was served by Mrs. Pat Clauer of Aurelia, close friend of the bride. . . . The dining room was tastefully decorated in yellow and white . . . with a large wedding bell suspended in the center."

Despite the newspaper's depiction, the wedding actually reflected basic simplicity. They could not afford to rent a hall, buy elaborate decorations, or hire a caterer. Here's how my mother reminisced about her wedding day some sixty years later: "A huge snowstorm developed the night before and a lot of people couldn't get through the snow and ice with their cars, horses, and buggies. Some who did manage to get there arrived late. Cars had no defrosters then so they used a kind of blow torch to keep frost off the windshield. The lilies in my bouquet wilted soon after we were in church. We were thankful for the small group that made it there, especially Rita and Vince, our wedding attendants. The cooks did manage to arrive and feed the ones able to come." True to form, my mother found something laudable in a situation that must have been disappointing. She could have whined about what happened but chose, instead, to find within the inadequate aspects the enjoyable things that kept her heart warm with gratitude.

When Mom spoke of her nanny-housekeeping years, she'd often concluded with, "I always wanted to live in a big house of my own." She never did. Not even when she could afford to do so much later in life. The old two-story, wooden-framed house that she and Dad moved into consisted of three bedrooms, a kitchen, and a living room. My brothers slept in one upstairs bedroom and we girls in the other. In summertime, the boys learned to exist with their buzzing companions, a hive of honey bees that took over a spot under the eaves.

My parents lived on rented land where Dad grew alfalfa, corn, and oats, while also raising cattle and pigs. Along with giving birth to eight children, Mom took care of cooking, laundry, cleaning, gardening and canning produce, childcare, sewing and mending, mowing a huge lawn, cow-milking, chicken-raising, and keeping the farm's financial ledgers.

Each day required constant labor. There was no indoor plumbing, and the youngest babies all wore cloth diapers. These smelly things had to be rinsed out in a bucket of water ("the diaper pail"), then washed in a hand-wringer tub and hung outdoors to dry. If any clothing required pressing, this was done with an iron heated on the top of the stove. And then there was feeding the family. Besides produce from a huge garden, Mom used every item of food available. Each summer she sent us older children to the nearby grove of trees to pick fruit from wild elderberry and chokecherry bushes. From these she produced delicious jellies and jams.

Inconvenience and privations abounded. One of these involved drinking water. A windmill in the pasture pumped water from the well into a pipe leading to a faucet south of the big red barn. That's where Mom walked, through a manure-laden cattle yard, to carry buckets of drinking water back to the house. If there was no wind, water from the well would not flow. Sometimes this proved disastrous, like the day she cooked a meal for the five men helping my father with the harvesting. This turned out to be one of the few times my mother fell apart, her inner mettle totally spent.

While Mom prepared the noon meal for these men, she ran out of cooking and drinking water. This presented an awful dilemma because there was no one to watch the three of us children, all under the age of six. She couldn't take us with her through the mucky cattle-yard but she had to get the water. "Finally, I just said a prayer, left Jerry (the oldest child) to watch you two, got the buckets and hurried down there. I couldn't believe it. Right when I got to the faucet, the wind stopped blowing. No water. I just stood there and cried."

It wasn't only drinking water that was hard to get. Water for washing clothes, bathing, and cleaning dishes came from a rain-water cistern next to the house. Priming the pump demanded a significant amount of pushing and pulling on the handle at the top of the cistern before water streamed forth.

There was, of course, no indoor plumbing. In frigid, winter weather, those trips to the outhouse felt twice as long. Besides this icy inconvenience, overnight chamber pots in the house needed emptying in the outhouse the next morning.

There were other household chores that were equally burdensome. The stove was fueled on corn cobs that had to be hauled in from their storage bins in a corner of the garage. The dirty, black coal that fired the living room stove came in huge chunks that had to be broken down in order to fit inside. With this endless stream of work and responsibilities, I wonder how my mother ever found time to sew. She proved to be an excellent seamstress, one of her proudest achievements being the stylish blue suit she made for herself. Since she couldn't afford to buy new material, she took apart one of my father's suits that no longer fit him and used that cloth instead.

When Mom was thirty-seven, she experienced an especially tough year. While still living in the century-old house, she was pregnant with a seventh child. This proved to be one of her most difficult pregnancies with several overnight stays in the hospital before the actual birth. A day after one of those times of hemorrhaging and pain, her father died of blood poisoning. She was too weak to attend the funeral, but in spite of how ill she felt, visitors who came for the funeral found hospitality and lodging at our home, along with meals that Mom prepared for them. It was during this year, too, that Dad caught his finger in a grain grinder that cut the end off of it. This led to a serious infection.

Mom must have struggled greatly as she faced those constant hardships. Yet, she did not give in to self-pity or resentment. She picked herself up and went on, day after day, year after year. In *Scarred by Struggle, Transformed by Hope*, Joan Chittister writes, "All struggle is not loss. All those who struggle do not give way to depression, to death of the spirit, to dearth of heart. We not only can survive struggle but, it seems, we are meant to survive in new ways, with new insights, with new heart."[2] It was not so much "a new heart" being created in my mother. Instead, a basic resilience deepened and a spirit that refused to let go of hope for better days became stronger.

I observed this at a time when disappointment crushed Mom's joy. She rarely owned anything new. After years of living with second hand items, excitement filled her voice when the first unused piece of furniture arrived: a stuffed, brown rocking chair. Her elation did not last long. Grandpa Wilberding came to visit soon after, lit his thick cigar and proceeded to carelessly burn a hole in the arm. As a young child who witnessed this disaster, I still remember Mom's utter frustration and dismay at that cigar burn.

She bounced back from the incident as she did from others. One source of maintaining her resiliency came from a love of the outdoors. This love nurtured and revived her spirit. In spite of the vigorous work, Mom relished living in the country. As a young girl, she grew to enjoy the vast space and the freedom of the rural area. When her family traveled to Dyersville to visit her grandparents, she found all sorts of opportunities for play on the farm's wide expanse.

When Mom was a fifth grader, her grandparents paid for the train tickets for her older brother Emil and her to travel to Dyersville. They stayed two months. A girl of similar age lived on a farm across the pasture. Everyday the two of them, Marcie and Hilda, met at the creek to play. Mom's voice always contained happiness when recounting her memories of that vacation: "It was the time I grew to love the farm. We'd go to the woods, pick berries and get scratched. We went swimming in the creek, wearing our black bloomers. That's the year I learned how to milk a cow."

The milking scene also included a bit of helping out. Her grandparents ran a dairy with many cows to be milked—by hand, of course. In the summertime, biting flies swarmed around the cows, and they kept slapping their tails to keep the irritating insects off. Grandpa Meyer asked the children to hold the swishing, manure-laden tails and keep them still so the milkers would not be hit in the face. He paid a penny for every tail the children held. Mom thought this to be a great bargain.

Learning how to milk a cow came in handy. When she married, Mom's dad gave her a cow as a gift. Mom milked this red roan with a certain trepidation because it always kicked when a cat came nearby. Consequently, she put hobbles called "kickers" around the cow's two back legs to keep from being hurt.

Mom laughed, her brown eyes sparkling, as she recalled another memory, "I also learned how to dance the Charleston that summer in Dyersville. Aunt Phine had me stand in a doorway, hands on opposite sides of it, and taught me how to swing."

Not until I was an adult did I know how much Mom enjoyed dancing. She told me about this one day when she found it difficult to get out of her chair due to stiff arthritic limbs. She followed that comment about dancing with, "Aunt Ida told me: 'Hilde, you'll be dancing into heaven.' I wonder what she'd think if she saw me now."

Mom's fondness for country life and the delight she experienced there in her younger years strengthened her durable nature. When she married, she not only endured the financial struggles and relentless hard work, she took pride in the abundance of her large garden. She also tried to help us enjoy the farm. When they stopped raising brooder chickens, Mom took the time and energy to clean out that small building and create a playhouse for my older sister and me. She looked back on that time with satisfaction and said, "I think I enjoyed doing that as much as you girls did." She also gave us all kinds of suggestions for games we could play in the grove. In the midst of hardship, my mother chose to seek joy and bring it to others whenever she could.

Her diaries confirm the satisfaction she received from being in creation's beauty. Every trip she and Dad took contains a brief comment about earth's beauty: "The canyon, a beautiful sight . . . lots of pretty pine trees . . . a

very scenic drive . . . trees along the river in full fall color
. . . stopped beside a babbling brook . . . watched three
dolphins playing in the river channel."

This appreciation of nature also benefitted Mom's spirit
in her later years when physical impairment confined her
to extended stays at home. She looked forward each day to
the magnificent sunsets which she easily viewed from her
living room chair. This scene brought her such immense
pleasure. Often, she would pick up the phone and call my
Aunt Rita or a next-door neighbor and urge them, "Look
out the window. The colors tonight are really gorgeous."

I've often thought of how much even a brief touch of
natural beauty serves to invigorate and enliven a drooping
spirit. It certainly did for my mother. Unfortunately,
elderly people who experience immobility are unable to
see out a window and rarely spend time outdoors. What
a difference it could make for their well-being if someone
took the time to push a wheelchair, or lend a steady arm
so the infirm could feel the fresh air and warm sun, listen
to birdsongs, and derive the pleasure that comes from
nature's beauty.

Even a small kindness makes a difference. Whenever
my mother recounted stories of early farm life, she rarely
spoke about the "tough stuff." Instead, she reminisced in a
grateful voice as she told of people like Dad's grandmother,
Josephine Kohns, bringing a wedding gift of a Plymouth
hen and twenty chicks so Mom could raise her own brood.
Grandma Kohns, an older widow, lived alone on her farm,
and Mom often invited her to Sunday dinner. Many times

she brought with her some useful gift like a rug, a pillow, or something else she had made. Those gifts added much joy to my mother's life.

The Wearts, an older couple who owned the farm my parents rented, also extended numerous kindnesses to our family. They brought Christmas gifts for us children and special food for the holidays. I think my mother remembered every kindness shown her. She carried that kindness forth to others. Never hesitant to find gratitude instead of grumbling, Mom's resilient spirit led her to look at what enriched her life rather than at what deprived it.

In my youth I believed my mother's inner strength could withstand whatever challenges arose. As I grew older, however, I wondered if she could weather adversities of spirit as well as she managed physical ones. When my next-youngest brother, David, drowned at the age of twenty-three, his death greatly challenged the core of her ability to bounce back. As with other difficult experiences, Mom managed to go on with life, refusing to be defeated by her sorrowing mother's heart, unaware this would not be the last significant loss to threaten her joy by a drowning tragedy.

Eight years later, on a fishing trip in Canada, my mother's two best women friends died in the lake they were bathing in, not far from the campground where she sat with my father and their husbands. She stared in shock and disbelief as the lifeless bodies of her beloved friends were brought back to shore. Those tragic deaths nearly crushed Mom's robust spirit. For over a decade, the drowning scene left her with horrific nightmares.

Adverse experiences can hone and strengthen innate resilience or they can infect this valuable quality with unresolved bitterness and anger. It is not uncommon to meet people who talk continually about hurts and misfortunes of the past. This bitterness keeps them from seeing and enjoying the good their lives currently hold.

Viktor Frankl wrote in *Man's Search for Meaning*: "Between a stimulus and response there is a space. In that space is our power to choose our response. In our response lies our growth and our freedom." My mother never knew Viktor Frankl's writing, but her attitude toward the difficult things in life attests to how she lived his philosophical beliefs. Rather than focus on the unwanted aspects, she chose to dwell on the worth within her life. This wisdom kept her spirit alive and positive as she aged.

CHAPTER 3

The SHADOW SIDE

The Mark of Unworthiness

Sometimes love
concedes excessively,
gives in too readily,
bows too low
when it ought to
stand upright.

Sometimes love
fails to face boldly
what threatens
to damage the light
within the clear soul.

Sometimes love
bends repeatedly
with submission,
not realizing
the damaging power
in patriarchal anger.

Sometimes love
turns the other cheek
in deference

when it needs to
raise the strong hand
of No More
and Stop This Now.

Sometimes love
fails in self-defense,
leaving in its place
the lasting mark
of unworthiness.

—Joyce Rupp

. . .You don't have to wait for someone to treat you
bad repeatedly. All it takes is once, and if they get away
with it that once, if they know they can treat you like
that, then it sets the pattern for the future.

—Jane Green
Bookends

Five years before my mother died, her brother-in-law Beryl
called to say, "Hilda, you are among the ten women I most
admire. I think you are remarkable." His comment amazed
her. She did not know what to do with that unexpected
affirmation. She could hardly accept she might be that
special, so unconfident was she of her own merit. Mom did
not take praise readily. When she was in her seventies, I tried
to affirm her constant generosity but she quickly dismissed
it with, "Oh, you're just putting me on a pedestal."

I never thought my mother to be remarkable until my
mid-forties, after Dad died. I always liked Mom but she
was "just my mother," doing the things a mother does. I
took so much for granted. I knew she would be there for
me, and she was. Along with that, I allowed myself to be
overly influenced by my father whose patriarchal voice
ruled our family.

That's what prompted Uncle Beryl's call. Mom married
his brother, a strong German farmer who loved her but also
verbally abused her, who rarely affirmed her intelligence
and continually overpowered her with his opinions and
decisions. He had the final say on everything. Mom checked
with him for approval when spending money, even on

her own clothes. Before she went anywhere, other than
the usual grocery and farm shopping, she looked for his
consent.

This male-controlled approach most certainly reflects
the culture of my parents' era, especially in rural America.
Men were expected to be in charge and have the final
word in whatever mattered. Not all males followed this
approach but, unfortunately, my father definitely fell into
that dominating pattern. It's not surprising that my mother
acquiesced to his judgments and choices in most everything.
What caused Dad's patriarchy to stand apart from that of
other husbands and fathers, however, was his explosive
anger accompanied by demeaning language. In spite of
her inner strength, Mom rarely stood up for herself when
these eruptions occurred.

Our best qualities have a shadow side to them. C.G.
Jung, the Swiss psychiatrist, who developed this concept,
named this aspect "the shadow" because each personality
quality that shines forth to others has an opposite, veiled,
"shadow" side. Jung taught that the shadow lies hidden in
our unconscious, either because we are unaware or because
we refuse to accept that we have this potential within us.

The shadow side of my mother's resiliency revealed itself
in her acquiescence and compliance. The one place where
her courageous spirit bowed low instead of standing up tall
was before my father. She let Dad be in charge, consented
to his constant claim to be right, allowed that his way was
best, and usually kept silent if she disagreed. Like a lot of
men in his time, he believed that only women were to be

in the kitchen. He never prepared any food—not even a piece of toast—didn't carry dishes to the sink, wouldn't think of washing them or even picking up something from the floor. Mom accepted this as the norm.

Although she was an excellent cook, the only way Dad complimented her on a delicious meal was to say, "Well, that didn't taste too bad." When she prepared something not to his liking, made a mistake with some task, or failed to follow through with his wants, he would often become irritated and yell, "Why did you do it that way?" and proceed to call her—or what she did—"stupid." I could see how deeply it affected Mom as she pulled back into herself with teary sadness in her eyes and a glum look on her face.

My mother never yelled back. She did not say, "I don't deserve that. I am *not* stupid." She did not demand that he treat her with respect. When she did give an explanation concerning the accusation, her voice sounded hurt, not angry or indignant. With each episode, Dad's emotional outburst eventually passed. He went on to act out of his better self while Mom meekly swallowed the resultant hurt. Resiliency did not serve her well in this regard. Her strength became her weakness. The shadow side came forth when she responded with an unhealthy willingness to submissively take the verbal blows that came her way.

Physical pain, loss of loved ones through death, struggles with finances—I doubt any of that affected Hilda more than how Lester treated her verbally. With all those years of being called "stupid," I understood why she failed to believe in her self-worth and brushed off affirmation when directed toward her.

Dad's parents did not allow him to go to high school; instead, he worked on their family's farm. Mom often remarked to us children "how smart" Dad was, telling us he received his education through reading a lot, which he did as an adult. Mom, on the other hand, graduated from high school with report cards carrying excellent scores. Consequently, Dad let her keep the farm's financial ledgers and write the checks. She enjoyed reading, developed great skill at crossword puzzles and anyone playing Scrabble with her met with a formidable challenge. Yet, Mom doubted her intellectual ability. This played out in numerous ways, such as avoiding certain books or conversations with the dismissive comment, "Oh, that's too deep for me."

In the years following Dad's death, Mom and I had many enriching talks during our travels together. Every once in a while the topic of her inability to believe in her self-worth entered into our conversation. On one of those occasions after we returned from a trip, I wrote the following in my journal:

> Always I am glad for our time together. Our good talk the other day about how she puts herself down. Mom talked about how poor they were; she had nothing. Developed a perfectionist way. Had to succeed at school. Told me how good she felt when she won over another girl with top scores in English. She knows she doesn't speak well of herself. She said, "I did a stupid thing"

about the bathroom fall. And the day before she said about giving me map directions, "Well, at least I got that right." So we talked about her comment. It felt good. I think we are better friends than ever.

Another time when I approached Mom about how disparagingly she spoke of herself, she reflected on her childhood, and that helped me to understand how Dad's verbal abuse added to a lack of self-esteem already embedded in her. Mom talked about her childhood in detail, how she was made fun of ("Your sister is crazy"— referring to Armella's epileptic seizures), how one boy always taunted her until she walloped him with her lunch box one day. She described her family's economic situation and how she felt she was ugly, not pretty like other girls. She did know she could do well in school, especially in English.

I assured Mom that it was not too late to change her belief about herself. She immediately responded, "I've changed a lot." I affirmed her and asked if she thought she could change further in the area of self-esteem. I then suggested her "homework" could be to write ten good things about herself. I went a bit too far with that suggestion because she immediately quipped, with an impish grin, "I'll never do it!"

I don't know if she wrote anything or not, but I do know that Mom's self-worth took a lot of battering from my father. As a child I experienced distress when I heard his angry outbursts, and even more so as I matured. Still, until my late thirties, I leaned emotionally toward Dad. As a youth, I worked outside with him on the farm where I felt most at home. And there were special times when I experienced his "better side," his ability to show love and kindness. When we were small children, Dad sat down after the evening meal to read and would make a place for one of us to be beside him in his easy chair. He leaned over every once in awhile, chuckled, and gave us a teasing "whisker rub." I cherished those times with my father.

Looking back, I believe Dad did his best to show affection. I felt close to him and admired his good qualities. When his anger issues took center stage, they blocked out the more likeable traits revealed in his work and social life, especially his keen sense of humor and adept story-telling that often left listeners responding with contagious laughter. Dad's integrity gave him a reputation as a valued businessman, an honest person who kept his word. Always a hard worker, he provided for our family, helped neighbors in need, and welcomed both friend and stranger into our home, including salesmen who came to visit. He pulled cars out of snowy ditches and stopped to help stranded travelers. He took them to get help and even gave them oil for their cars. One autumn he and my brother Roger went to the farm of a neighbor who was incapacitated with cancer. They spent several days harvesting his corn fields. The neighbor wanted to pay but Dad replied, "No, you don't owe us anything. We wanted to do this for you."

Dad could also listen and be compassionate. Mom told of a lady in town who was "very slow mentally and had lots of trouble in the past. She had a child taken from her because of abuse and neglect." She used to call Mom, wanting to get together for coffee. In wondering what she might do, Mom explained the situation to Dad, "I think she just needs a friend." To which he responded, "Is there any reason why you can't do that?"

While my father could be sympathetic and thoughtful, he could also be exceedingly hardhearted. Mom did not like to fish very much and Dad knew it. Still, he demanded she go with him—and she dutifully did. All he wanted to do, as Mom put it, was "fish, fish, fish." She did enjoy the scenery—the beauty of the lake, the woods, the birds, the wide sky. Sometimes she'd sit in the boat gazing at the sight, perfectly content. Before long Dad would growl, "Pick up your pole and fish. That's what we came for!" And so she would.

One summer they went on one of their usual trips to Manitoba, Canada. On the first day of fishing, swarms of gnats hung in clusters, flying in their faces and biting them. Mom didn't know until the evening how allergic she was to these insects. Her face, arms, and legs swelled to red lumps of gigantic proportion, painful to the touch and incredibly itchy. The next morning she begged off going out in the boat but Dad insisted, goading her with, "Get fishing. We didn't travel all this way for nothing." He insisted she be out on the lake that entire, miserable week even though she longed to stay in the cabin and rest. In spite of this, she still prepared the lunches and evening meals. When Mom spoke about this, I felt sad for her, the way I did in my youth when I watched her tolerate Dad's temperamental flare-ups and insistence on ultimate authority.

My mother practiced endurance and chose carefully when she challenged my father's way of doing things. When she did, it was almost always on behalf of someone other than herself, such as when one of us children needed something she felt was good for us, or when it seemed imperative the two of them attend a social event he wanted to avoid.

The shadow side of resiliency shows itself in a person accepting too much, swallowing what ought to be spat out, tolerating ridicule rather than facing conflict, and refusing to put an end to what produces harm. My mother's situation reflected this. She kept receiving Dad's insulting language, accepting and living with this harshness even when it created a canyon of unworthiness in her.

Why? Besides the fact that patriarchy was an acceptable social norm, my mother loved my father. One day after Dad died she turned her thoughts to memories of their courtship, telling me, "I fell for him on the first date. There was never anyone else, although I dated others. I never stopped loving him." That day Mom also shared some of her intimate memories, including how she sat on Dad's lap the night before her wedding and felt such happiness.

Mom also told of a night when they were dating, how she anticipated some cozying up on the porch swing but her sister Armella sat on the porch steps and kept staring at the two of them. Mom signaled her with "one of those annoying looks" indicating she ought to get out of there, but Armella just sat all the tighter. "She made me so mad,"

Mom said. "Finally your Dad had to leave so he could get to work the next day at the windmill plant in Sioux City." This initial love for Lester remained firmly planted in Hilda's heart the entirety of their married life.

Even after Dad died, Mom rarely spoke about the unkind way he treated her. She stuffed that pain away too tightly for it to dislodge easily. It happened, too, that Dad mellowed somewhat after retirement. We children were surprised to learn some of the changes that came about, ("What, Dad washed the windows and went to buy groceries?!") but the edge of patriarchy remained too deeply ingrained to be dissolved completely. During this same period, Mom really needed a knee replacement; the severe pain was such that she could hardly walk. Dad insisted she "live with it." And she did until after his death several years later.

I hesitated writing this chapter about my father's verbal abuse because of my affection for him and because I did not want others to think less of my dad. At the same time, I believe that my mother's experience of this abuse yields an essential insight into her resilient nature. During the time I faced making a decision about this, a confirmation to include this aspect came to me by way of a phone conversation with one of Dad's sisters. When I mentioned writing a memoir about Mom she instantly responded with, "And what are you going to do about Lester?" This aunt, along with others in his family, knew how harsh Lester could be with Hilda and wondered how she continually put up with it. They admired Mom for how she managed to be such a gracious woman in spite of the quick outbursts of anger and self-righteousness foisted upon her.

Mom paid a price for doing so. She suffered greatly from arthritis from age forty onward. Research indicates that one cause of this condition can be from the emotion of unresolved anger taking up residence not only in one's spirit but in one's physical being as well. I do wonder about this in light of the verbal abuse my mother experienced. If she had been able to voice her distress she might not have carried the anger in her bones and experienced so much physical debilitation later in life.

Abuse is never acceptable and ought not to be tolerated under any circumstance. My mother accepted my father's approach as a part of being 'the faithful wife.' This delusional acceptance derived not only from the norm of patriarchy but also from their ethnic background. Both of my parents entered marriage influenced by their German heritage. Mom's side of the family was beer-drinking, fun-loving, easy-going folks while most of Dad's thrived on hard work, inflexible opinions, and financial success.

Dad's Germanic advice and commands rang out loudly. How many times I heard one of the following remarks:

> Do it the way I told you.
>
> You're too big for your britches.
>
> If you want to eat here, you're going to work here.

If I told you once, I told you a hundred times, *this* is how you do it.

You're going to get a big head, Smarty Pants.

You're going to keep at that job until it's finished.

Do it right the first time.

Stop running around like a chicken with its head cut off.

If you have a problem, *you* figure it out.

Stop that bawling or I'll give you something to bawl about.

Quit whining.

Don't go feeling sorry for yourself.

Sometimes Dad's beliefs fueled Mom's way of thinking and speaking to us, but her approach lacked his strong forcefulness. She could get angry and did not tolerate bad behavior, but when she corrected us it sounded quite different from Dad's hostility.

Besides absorbing verbal abuse, yet another shadow side of resiliency resided in my mother. It had to do with offering compassion and kindness to herself. Sorrow never seemed to be far from her doorstep. She treated it in a manner similar to how she responded to my father's insults, believing, in her words, that "you go on with what you have to do, no matter how hard it is. You just learn to accept and get over it."

Even at my brother's funeral she held back her tears, except at the closing of the casket lid. An ingrained message—"Be strong!"—pushed those unwept tears back inside. The tough Germanic spirit Mom acquired worked in reverse when it came to dealing with her own suffering. "Being strong" meant not allowing kindness to herself.

When physical pain dominated her later years of life, I often wished that Mom would have indicated more often how much she hurt. Unlike some older people who speak constantly about their aches and pains, my mother chose not to do this. Had she done so, we could have comforted and supported her more fully and also sought medical relief sooner. Instead, she generally chose to keep silent, influenced by a history of approaching pain of body and spirit in a compliant or long-suffering way.

If Mom had listened to and tended that which pained her deeply, it could have eased a lot of inner heartache and freed her much sooner from its burden. But that was not Hilda Rupp's way. To this day I am astounded that my mother did not become an embittered, resentful old woman.

The reality is that she became just the opposite.

CHAPTER 4

The BATHTUB QUESTION

Turning Away, Turning Toward

These golden days of summer
grow threadbare with the first
tattered browns of autumn.

Everything green begins to sink
back into the earth
with seeming ease and abandon.

Tall, stiff stems bend low,
grasses lie down in surrender,
and the last of the harvest laughs
at the settled winter to come.

Like old age, one can only water
wilting plants for so long
before they grow dull and shapeless
with the coming season,
can only urge persistent plentitude
until the source is completely spent.

Everywhere the voice of yielding
echoes in the bones of elderhood,
cries out in a frail voice to be heard
and given a welcome domicile.

How to accept the changing season,
to enter fully the hills and valleys
turning toward completion,

how to convince the
mind and heart to stop clutching
previous contentment?

—**Joyce Rupp**

"I am a foreigner in the land of old age
and have tried to learn its language . . ."

—**May Sarton**
Coming Into Eighty

It's uncanny how one little phrase, spoken nonchalantly, can trigger a deluge of memories. Ten years after Mom's death, during my stay as an overnight guest with a family I did not know, a simple question jolted me back into her aging process. My housing had been arranged by the coordinator of an evening event where I was scheduled to speak. A few hours before the talk, my hostess drove me to her home. Once we arrived, she invited me to follow her upstairs to the room I would be using. As we passed the open door to the bathroom she paused before it, looked at me and asked, "Will you be taking a shower?" When I responded "yes," her next question startled me: "Can you get your legs over the bathtub?"

Irritation quickly leapt inside of me. I couldn't believe her question. I wanted to defend myself with, "You better believe I can. I walk three miles every day." Instead, I kept my mouth shut and meekly mumbled, "Yes, no problem."

Left alone in the guest bedroom, indignation continued to jolt my usually calm self. "What a condescending question," I muttered as I hung a few clothing items on empty hangers. Then I sat down, took some deep breaths in an effort to be less emotionally charged and reviewed the scene. My hostess appeared to be twenty-five years younger. She undoubtedly viewed me as I did my mother when we had a similar age difference. Looking back, I recalled thinking of Mom as "old" ever since her mid-fifties. This awareness eased my bruised ego but the slap of the question definitely woke me up. The sting finally left some days later when I laughed about it with my mutually aged friends.

As if to rub salt into the wound, the following week I was out for my daily walk on a trail which included a winding, steep hill. As I reached the top without a lot of huffing and puffing I met a well-muscled jogger at least twenty years younger. He greeted me with a smile and "good job" as he passed by. Instead of feeling pleased with his affirmation, I immediately mused, "Would he have said that if I were his age?"

About that time I read an essay by Maya Angelou in *Even the Stars Look Lonesome* in which she confronts the reality of her aging. Angelou's honest assessment of her body's startling changes moved me a bit closer to acknowledging my own. She writes: "At sixty my body, which had never displayed a mind of its own, turned obstreperous, opinionated and deliberately treacherous. The skin on my thighs became lumpy, my waist thickened and my breasts— It's better not to mention them at all except to say that they seemed to be in a race to see which could be first to reach my knees."[1]

I didn't want to think I was at that stage of aging but awareness of being treated like "an old lady" bounded into view again a few months later. My cousin's thirty-something son described a book he liked. He then added, "It's quite dense, but I think you could manage it." Oh, how I wanted to hurl a sarcastic comment. Instead, I swallowed and said under my breath, "Just because I have graying hair doesn't mean I've lost my ability to understand what I read."

That same day I attended an outdoor wedding. This included a walk up a steep, graveled hill. As I began the climb, a younger friend's husband turned to me and asked, "Need an arm?" He said it with such kindness that, even though I could have managed fine by myself, I linked arms with him and up we went. "Way to go," I said to myself, noting that I was really working on accepting other people's view of myself as "elderly" and being more helpless than I actually felt.

Those experiences helped me see why younger people proffer patronizing comments toward their elders when they are actually trying to be caring and helpful. I recall saying to a dear cousin when she joined in a walk for cancer, "Oh, you manage so well for being eighty years old." Being the gracious woman she was, Elva only smiled. Now I wonder what she felt about my thoughtless remark.

In many ways I've unknowingly spoken with condescension or acted in a demeaning manner toward people in their later years with comments like "Can't believe you're ninety-two," "You look so good for your age," or "Are you still driving?" I found myself doing this when I stopped to visit Mom while she lunched with her card club. Among the "old gals" was a friend in her mid-nineties. Because Meals on Wheels delivered lunches to my mother, I tried to make conversation by asking this friend if she received them. Her indignant "no" immediately set me straight about that misconception.

The bathtub question led me to reflect on how I treated Mom as she aged. It took her a while to accept her growing limitations. Now I understand better how she struggled with her bodily changes, signals given by the little queries and comments she made regarding herself. At age eighty-one, she turned to me as we left the house and asked, "Do I walk old?" On another occasion, before we went to a social event, she turned and urged, "You be sure to tell me if I ever have bad breath, won't you?" She was also uneasy about having spots and stains on her clothes—something that seems to become a regular habit of older people who can easily drop some food item on themselves.

During the last five years of Mom's life, I valued our talks about her physical decline. One day she commented, "I think I've really aged this year, don't you?" I said I couldn't tell. It was *her* body. How did she feel about it? In response, she spoke about feeling tired a lot and less able to be as active as in the past. But no matter how much my mother tried to explain what it felt like to be aging at an ever quickening pace, I did not grasp that reality very well.

How did I treat my mother as someone who was "old"? I tried to do too much for her. Overly eager to show my love and lessen what I considered her physical burdens, I attempted to do all I could to alleviate anything that seemed difficult. I was oblivious to how my well-meant desire to help actually added to her sense of inadequacy and infringed on her ability to do things for herself.

On one of my visits Mom surprised me by refusing my offer to dust her bedroom. "We older people need to do all we can for ourselves," she explained in a determined but kindly way. Her comment opened my constricted view on aging. Without stating it explicitly, she was saying, "I need this. I feel good about myself when I can still do something. Allow me to have this gift." From that time on I tried to back off of my pushiness and ask what kind of assistance she might need, instead of charging in and doing things she could accomplish herself.

Unfortunately, in my eagerness to make life easier for Mom I forgot this lesson from time to time. Several years after my offer to dust, I came to celebrate her eighty-third birthday and decided to clean the kitchen. Previous to her becoming progressively infirm, she kept a meticulous, tidy house. I noticed the last time I visited how grimy the kitchen cupboards were, especially the bottom shelves that were impossible for her to reach.

After my arrival, I announced that as part of her birthday gift I'd clean those cupboards, presuming she'd be elated. Instead, there was little response from her. Nevertheless, the next morning I went ahead with the work. I felt pleased about what I was doing as she sat nearby in the living room, her ankles swollen over the sides of her shoes. I could tell by the rasping sound I heard that she found it difficult to breathe.

After about a half hour, Mom called out to me, "Do you know how this makes me feel?"

I got up off my knees, went into the living room and sat down beside her. Then, instead of asking how she felt, I sermonized, insisting she accept my help: "You worked so hard raising us eight children. Now it's my opportunity to return something to you by cleaning the cupboards."

I shoved other thoughts and notions at her. I even asked her to think how she'd have felt if her mother had lived to be eighty-three—wouldn't she have wanted to do the same for her? On and on I preached.

After my egotistical, insensitive proclamations, Mom tried again to get me to listen: "Put yourself in my place. Here I am, not having any energy, staying in bed late in the morning while you work in the kitchen. I sit in my chair while you get the meals." She spoke those words with such a distressful tone.

I thought I was tuned in. "Yes, Mom, I need to hear what you're saying. I do understand. I'm very independent, too."

Well, I didn't understand. And I *still* didn't listen. I went on and on about all the past hardships she endured. When I finally finished, she snapped, "You don't owe me anything!"

"But Mom, I don't do this because I owe it to you. I do it because I love you."

"Well then," she replied, backing down, "You're not like most people. They don't have that attitude."

My aging mother kept trying to have me hear her pain. I didn't. Finally, I concluded, "But I love to do this for you. I feel so good being able to help." (Another ego statement. It made *me* feel good, not her.) I thanked Mom for our talk and went back to working. Only after she died did I realize her acute experience of feeling weak, worthless, and sad that day. How distraught she felt over the humbling limitations that physical frailty brings. My insistence on "helping" only added to her sense of this. It was okay to thank her for all she did in the past, but much more importantly, she really wanted a listening heart. She didn't give a damn about those cupboards.

I wish now that I had sat down by my mother and said, "This must be really hard for you. What's it like to be able to do so little? How would you like me to be with you as you go through this? What would you like me to do now?" And I would truly listen, listen, listen.

About eight years after this conversation, I read an article by Dr. Rachel Naomi Remen in which she refers to the difference between helping and serving. This distinction clarified a lot. When we aim to "help," Remen explains, the other person feels less than an equal. The "helper" comes across as the strong one while the one who's being helped feels weak. By thinking we are doing something worthy, she explains, we may actually be diminishing "their self-esteem, their sense of worth, integrity and wholeness." Remen suggests that, instead of an attitude of "I'm helping you," we approach our care for another as service to one who is our equal, not someone in need. [2]

What I didn't understand when I was trying to help Mom is that when I set out to help, I immediately put myself in the position as the one holding energy and strength. Had I listened to the deeper layer of her words, the place inside of her that ached because of limited physical ability, she would have been comforted, knowing her pain had been heard. She would not have felt alone in her suffering.

From my experience with my mother, I learned how swiftly we search for what to do for our loved ones when they hurt from aging's impediments. We do this not only to have them feel better, but to release some of our discomfort about their situation. Thus, we figure out ways to help them, but sometimes our help is mostly a nuisance, something they put up with to make *us* feel better. For example, it is *we* who decide they need to get out of the house when they are perfectly content to not go anywhere. (Do we have any notion of the energy it might take to do this sort of thing?) Granted, there are times when older persons need that nudge to be more socially engaged, but a lot of times it makes *us* feel better, not them. We miss this reality because they smile graciously in a most conciliatory way and act like we did them the biggest favor.

I recall encouraging Sister Evangelista, a ninety-three-year-old member of my religious community, to accept her niece's invitation to fly to California for a visit. When she replied, "I just don't do that anymore," I thought, "Oh, she's missing a great opportunity." I was unaware of the difficulty of travel for her, as well as being away from a comfortable, daily routine. Similarly, a mid-eighties friend recently commented, "My children don't get it. They think I should travel to visit them. I don't have *traveling energy* in me anymore. If they'd just ask me what *I* want, I'd tell them."

There are times when an aged person *does* want to go somewhere, but not where *we've* decided. Yes, she used to love ballgames, but now she dreads the thought of sitting all that time with stiff bones creaking in resistance, or worse, like one of my senior friends, he experiences the embarrassment of having to get up a number of times to use the restroom. Maybe dining at a restaurant used to bring great pleasure, but now it's mostly frustrating due to a hearing loss. (How can a hearing-impaired person convince those with excellent hearing that it's de-energizing and irritating to sit there and not catch half of what's being said in a noisy restaurant?)

Most people in elderhood enjoy a visit, but they tire quickly so it's best to keep visits short, and come back sooner. Mom used to love having company. In her later years she could keep up for a day or two when relatives from out of town visited, but she needed her own space and time to rest. If she did not have this, she would be frazzled for days afterward.

So the question is: "When to be of service and when to stand back and let older people do things on their own?" This decision involves regular discernment. No "one size fits all." Each day can be different than the one before. All might be well one visit and not the next. A time came when Mom needed assistance getting in and out of the car. Initiating this before she required help would have hurt her pride and kept her from feeling confident about being able to manage on her own.

Actually, if my mother were still alive, I'd probably be mumbling "sorry" a lot. I remember taking her to the supermarket. She only needed a few items but wanted to be able to choose them herself—a good thing for her to do. When we went into the store, she took a cart and started to walk slowly down the aisle. I intoned, "Mom, why don't you take one of those little baskets? It goes a lot faster." She turned toward me and patiently explained, "It's my back. It doesn't hurt quite so bad if I have a cart to lean on. Plus, it helps me keep my balance."

Another way I treated Mom as "an old person" was by giving advice she didn't need. How arrogant of me to believe I knew more than she did, even simple things like how to take her medicine. One morning I noticed she took her handful of pills by tossing them in her mouth and swallowing all of them with one gulp. "Don't do that," I warned, "It's not good for you." She just gave me one of those little smiles of hers that implied: "You can talk all you want to but I'll do it my way, anyhow." She did. And I don't think it made any difference.

As much as I tried to support my mother as she aged, I fell into the approach that other adult children do, treating an elder as a child. This especially pertained to Mom's diet. Because of numerous health issues, her physician insisted she be on a low-sugar, low-salt, low-fat diet. That was tough. My mother *loved* barbecue and fatty foods. And she didn't like being told what to eat. However, as she grew older she pretended to agree with watching her diet. I would carefully prepare healthy foods and take them on my visits, suggesting she put the food packets in her freezer, which she faithfully obliged me by doing. When I returned a month later, if I happened to look in the freezer, most of those foods were still there. (As I look back now, I bet the ones not in there had been thrown out.)

I didn't want my mother eating sugary foods and having to lose a foot or a limb to diabetes. I didn't want her consuming too much salt and having a stroke due to high blood pressure. But was my mother's health the *real* concern? Or was it the more probable realization of how much would be asked of *me*, how she would require more attention and how difficult it would be to provide for her needs? I wonder about that. I wonder if a person with only a few more years to live ought to be able to *enjoy* what they eat instead of denying themselves this satisfaction.

The day Mom died I went to her condo to meet with some of my siblings as we prepared the details for her funeral. I walked into the kitchen and smelled barbecue. I opened up the refrigerator and found a container with the remainder of the pork. I smiled and said out loud, "Good for you, Mom. I'm glad you had a delicious last meal."

How much do we protect older people by guarding them from certain foods, or moving them from their homes so they don't leave stove burners on, or taking their car keys away so they avoid an accident? When do we begin lending our voice regarding their medical procedures? These are not easy decisions. An older friend of mine remarked recently, "I'm preparing to move from my townhouse to a place that has independent, assisted, and fulltime care so my children won't have to make that decision for me in the future." Blessed are the children whose parents, like this one, make those choices while they are still able.

Because adult children have a tendency to take over their elderly parents' lives, it is not surprising that these parents often refrain from speaking about certain incidents. In her last years, Mom fell down in her home more often than she admitted. I sometimes heard about this from one of her friends who let it slip out in conversation. Mom might tell me about it, but only months later. More than one older friend of mine has mentioned taking a spill, having a memory glitch that might have involved serious consequences, or almost hitting someone while backing out of a parking place. They relate these things in a low voice, adding "I never tell my kids about this," fearing their freedom to choose and make decisions will be snatched away.

Sometimes our elders are in denial about their aging impairments but they have every right to be heard and respected, even if they are not capable of making the final decision. Each time any of my siblings or I stepped back and let our mother make necessary decisions regarding her health and well-being, we allowed her still to be in charge of her life. I did not realize at the time what a much needed gift of confidence this gave her.

Moving into acceptance of old age takes time, both for the aged person and the one who cares about him or her. It took quite awhile for me to truly understand and accept Mom's movement into a more physically-limited sphere of life. Only gradually did I accept the reality that the resilient and ever-energetic mother of mine could not do what used to be a natural part of her life. Now that I do understand more of what it is like to age, I cringe inside when I hear younger persons chiding older ones: "move faster," "stand up straight," "stop repeating," "pay attention," "don't eat that," "speak more clearly." I long to have them slip inside the skin of someone whose youthfulness has passed them by.

And I long to have my aged mother here again, so I could be kinder and more understanding.

CHAPTER 5

Fly WHILE YOU STILL HAVE *Wings*

Fly

Fly, fly
while you still
have wings.

Fly with buoyancy.
Do not falter in fervor
or waver in eagerness.

Lift off with a zestful spirit.

Enter fully what remains
of the fleeting,
diminishing years of life.
Do not wait
to follow what the heart
truly desires.

Fly now.

Take yourself
out the door into fresh
freedom.

Celebrate what awaits.
Spend yourself
like there's no tomorrow,

because there may be
no tomorrow.

Open your heart
to receive
latent possibilities of joy
and loving, lasting memories.

Fly, fly, fly,
while you still
have wings.

—Joyce Rupp

I thought my fireplace dead
and stirred the ashes.
I burned my fingers.

—Antonio Machado
Border of a Dream

An elderly person often contains a lot of fire amid what appears as dead ashes. My mother's eagerness to enjoy life convinced me of that. As an energetic woman she worked hard most of her life and rarely wavered in being active. In her younger years Mom rose at dawn and entered the day with a sense of purpose. As she aged, her body lost considerable vigor, but her spirit remained far from being a fading ember. In her seventies and eighties, she explored new vistas, expanded in openness where she had previously held bias, and nurtured beneficial relationships. Although somewhat quieter the final two years, she continued to be a celebrator of life.

All this didn't "just happen." A zest for life emblazoned itself on her spirit gradually. The initial source of this zest sprang from her family's ability to celebrate even when times were most bleak. Her father, my Grandpa Joe Wilberding, had a reputation for being "a jolly one." He regularly invited people to the house to play cards and enjoy one another's company. Entertainment included music and dancing. The house did not have a lot of space, but her dad moved the dining room table so the guests could move around. The children picked up his enthusiasm, and Della sent away for dance instructions so they could learn the steps. What fun

Della, Hilda, and the other children had as they practiced dancing.

The family's love of music filtered through various parts of their lives. Even though Mom sang songs like the "Tennessee Waltz" and "My Happiness" to us when we were small children, I did not know how much her early years included music until she told me about one of her high school experiences: "In eleventh grade, a telephone company man took a group of us girls to Sioux City. We sang a German song on the radio." At eighty-two Mom could still recall the words to that song, along with the happy occasion of their being taken to a restaurant for dinner afterward.

Socializing flowed in Mom's blood. Being part of a large, extended family certainly contributed to an enthusiasm for meeting people and entertaining them. In the years after her mother's death, her father's generous welcome of others into their home influenced this sense of hospitality. Mom spoke admiringly of him: "Even though there were many mouths to feed, Dad let us have our friends come over anytime. He seldom refused anyone who wanted to stay overnight with us."

After her marriage, many a party took place in my parents' old farm house. With no television and the Internet still a feature of science fiction, entertainment centered around baseball games, joke telling, card playing, eating, and drinking. Mom didn't imbibe much, but she enjoyed the company and had a good time. Of course, she cleaned the house beforehand, prepared the food, and took care of the messy cleanup. She described those parties more than once, how the next morning she found her younger brothers with their hangovers collapsed in sleep just about anywhere in the house, the air filled with cigarette and cigar smoke, along with the stale odor of whiskey and beer. Still, she relished those gatherings and counted them as part of her happy memories.

When we were young children Mom kept us busy with tasks and chores of all sorts in the summer months. She enticed us to do them by holding out the reward of future fun, like going to the local outdoor theater or a trip to Lake Okoboji for the carnival rides.

Relatives and friends enjoyed Mom and knew she liked to have a good time. This continued as she grew older. She wasn't about to sit around and stagnate. Gail Godwin's description in *The Finishing School* reminds me of the vibrancy in my mother's spirit:

> Death is not the enemy. Age is not the enemy. These things are inevitable. They happen to everybody. But what we ought to fear is the kind of death that happens in life. It can happen at any time you're going along, and then, at some point, you congeal. You know, like jelly. You're not fluid any more. You solidify at a certain point and from then on your life is doomed to be a repetition of what you have done before. That's the enemy. There are two kinds of people walking around on this earth. One kind you can tell just by looking at them at what point they

congeal into their final selves. It might be a very nice self, but you know you can expect no more surprises from it. Whereas, the other kind keep moving, changing. With these people you can never say X stops here, or now I know all there is to know about Y.[1]

Congealing never happened to Mom. She continually sought ways to enter into life as fully as possible. If there was an award for Queen of Hospitality, my mother surely would have received it. More than any other quality, this is what people remember about Hilda Rupp. They still marvel at her unwavering welcome of guests, how she put a delicious meal on the table with seeming ease an hour after unexpected visitors arrived.

This did not prevent her from sitting and visiting with them. Appearing as an irritated or anxious "Martha" did not play a part of my mother's presence with guests. At some point in the conversation, she slipped out quietly and busied herself in the kitchen. Then, as if by magic, food appeared and they were called to a table filled with hearty nourishment. Even when she grew frailer in body, Mom continued to welcome company eagerly although she no longer had the ability to prepare a meal for them.

This hospitality extended beyond home and into social relationships. Her address book bulged with a long list of correspondents. Whether she became acquainted with someone on a Canadian fishing trip, during a winter stay at Port Isabel in southern Texas, or at some social function, she usually added those contacts to her address book. Mom valued those relationships and corresponded regularly with a number of them.

Mom rarely missed sending a card for birthdays and anniversaries. She also wrote to people who were ill, including those she barely knew. My friend Janet recently reminded me of that. Mom did not know Janet personally but after I spoke of her hospitalization for serious back surgery, Mom asked for my friend's address. True to her caring and kindness, in the mail went a card: "Dear Janet, I am Joyce's mother. I know you are friends. I wanted to tell you that I am praying for you. I hope you recover soon, Yours truly, Hilda."

Besides the revitalization of spirit that Mom received from relationships, a good sense of humor added to her love of life. It kept her sane and resilient, especially in troublesome times. In *Journeywell*, Trish Herbert notes the value of humor for those in their senior years: "Being able to laugh at ourselves and at life makes life far more enjoyable. This ability to lighten up comes naturally for some of us. It happens to others after they've been roughed up by life a bit; they learn the hard way that they simply don't have enough energy 'to sweat the small stuff' and that it feels better to let go of some of the intensity and start being gentler with ourselves. Look for the humor and the silliness in what you hear, see, and read."[2]

Older people who maintain a sense of humor enter the unwanted changes of body and mind with much less tension and irritation. I found this to be true when Mom's wit eased distressful hospital situations. No one knew she was allergic to the morphine administered for her pain. This resulted in horrific nightmares and strange dreams. During this time, Mom kept telling the nurses she "went to New York." Once the effects of the morphine lessened, she joked to visitors about the "vacation" she took the night before, laughing at the absurdity of that hallucination.

Another time, this one in Cherokee Memorial Hospital, Mom awoke in the middle of the night to see a skinny, naked man standing in the doorway. His presence alarmed and frightened her. She quickly pushed the call button and nurses came to help the elderly man with dementia back to his room. The next day Mom chuckled as she joked about the incident, saying, "My boyfriend came for a visit last night."

Even when not in a troublesome situation, her humor lifted spirits. My sister Jeanne sat in Mom's hospital room one day while they worked on the daily crossword puzzle. They didn't get it completed so the next morning when Jeanne returned she brought the puzzle and continued asking Mom for answers to the clues. For each one, Mom got the correct word right away. Jeanne was amazed. When she looked up, she saw a little smirk on our mother's face. That was when she noticed Mom looking at the current newspaper—which contained the answers to yesterday's puzzle.

Mom's ability to laugh at herself kept self-pity away. As a belated eightieth birthday gift, my sister Sue and I took Mom to the Henry Doorly Zoo in Omaha. When I stopped in front of the entrance area, Sue went to get a wheelchair.

While Sue did that, Mom insisted she didn't need help getting out of the car, so I let her open the door and get out by herself. I looked ahead briefly for signs to the parking lot and when I looked back, there was no sign of Mom. Where could she have disappeared so quickly? I leapt out of the car and rushed around it. There she was, lying on the sidewalk next to the car, the result of her weak ankle giving way. As Sue and I helped her get up, Mom brushed herself off and made light of the incident, quipping, "There I go, falling for you again."

She was such a good sport about that embarrassing moment and similar ones, like the time she came to visit me while I lived in Colorado. Rain poured steadily the day she arrived. I wasn't concerned about pushing her in a wheelchair from the airline gate to the parking area outside, but I wondered how I would also manage her purse, small bag, and large suitcase. It turned out to be a rather hilarious scene: Mom in the chair, purses and bag on her lap, holding the umbrella—and me pushing the wheelchair, while also pulling the suitcase alongside. Again, she laughed about it, instead of being anxious or embarrassed.

There were numerous opportunities for my mother to laugh at herself. She learned early in life to see the ridiculous in upsetting situations, rather than give in to negativity. As a young boy, my older brother Jerry accompanied Mom in their 1940 Plymouth to take lunch to Dad in the field where he was planting corn. When she went to back up, she caught the car's bumper on a wire fence. No matter how she tried, she couldn't loosen the car. Dad had to drive off the cornfield and un-pry the stuck bumper from the fence. He grumped about taking the time to do that, but Mom thought it rather funny.

Then, there was the year Mom identified a plant in her garden as a volunteer tomato. She tended this healthy plant carefully, even put a fence around to support the stalk when it grew three feet and became wobbly. Imagine her dismay when she finally learned that the "tomato plant" was just an old "pig-weed," the common bane of corn fields. This, too, she could eventually laugh about and tell the story to others.

Mom never did learn how to say certain words with a foreign origin. When we laughed at her mispronunciations, she would just smile. *Hors d' oeuvres* were always "horse dee orveez," jalapeño peppers were "jolla lappa peenos," and a Grand Prix car was "a grand Pricks." Her challenges with pronunciation did not reflect a lack of intelligence. Saying a word correctly didn't matter much compared to the greater tasks and interests that were hers. Mom never tried to put on airs. "Accept life for what it is. Laugh at your own foibles when you can." That was my mother.

Playing games of any type sparked Mom's energy. As a child, the Christmas gifts included one family board game each year. Her dad enjoyed these as much as the children. It's no surprise, then, that whenever her grandchildren came to visit, out they went with Grandma to the kitchen table. She could sit there for hours and never be bored, playing checkers, UNO, canasta or some other competitive game with them. Of all the ones Mom played, Scrabble reigned as her favorite. I tried in every way possible to beat her at that game but rarely succeeded, even on the days when she might not recall what day it was or the details of who said what.

Her ability to play and have fun never ceased. In Mom's mid-seventies, an ice storm knocked out the heat and electricity. Fortunately, my sister Jeanne and husband Steve, along with their two children, were visiting at the time. I learned later how much she enjoyed their company during the storm. True to form, they played all sorts of games by candlelight and when they tired of that, they created stories of mystery and intrigue. Instead of experiencing impatience, fear or irritation with the storm, they enjoyed one another with laughter and amusement during the blustery evening.

The challenge of board games probably led to what became the most satisfying and zest-filled entertainment of her last ten years: "going to the boat," Mom's euphemism for gambling at a casino on the Missouri river. She went at least twice a month and always sounded more alive when she mentioned having been there. Even with a minimum amount of energy to walk, she almost always leapt at the chance to "go to the boat." She kept her gambling wings aloft as long as she could. Three days before her death, she caught one last ride and enjoyed a final visit to her favorite haunt.

Sometimes Mom defended her enjoyment of this entertainment with "I don't smoke, drink, or go to dances, or spend a lot of money eating out. Besides, I only take a certain amount of money. When it's gone, it's gone." Actually, this enthusiastic lady brought good luck with her and usually came home with more money than she spent.

Those trips to the casino developed slowly. After working endlessly on the farm and constantly yielding to Dad's preferences, I watched with fascination as Mom started spreading her long-closed wings, inching her way toward greater freedom socially, beginning in her late fifties. This change took place after a car accident that could have proved fatal. Fortunately, it resulted in minor scrapes and bruises when she swerved to avoid an animal on the road, went into a ditch and through a fence. This event served to jolt loose a latent desire in Mom to live life to the fullest. What a momentous day when she announced, "Lester, I'm going to a card party this afternoon. Your lunch is ready. All you need to do is warm it in the microwave." When she told me about this, it was like hearing her wings take flight.

After that car accident, Mom entered into the "active aging" described by Joan Chittister in *The Gift of Years*: "There are two approaches to aging: passive aging and active aging. Passive aging gives way to the creeping paralysis of the soul that goes with the natural changes of the body. This kind of aging sees this last stage of life as a time in the throes of slow death rather than a time to live differently— and dauntlessly. Active aging cooperates with the physical effects of age by adjusting to a change of pace. . . . Active aging requires us to go on living life to the full no matter how differently."[3]

Hilda Wilberding at her graduation
from St. Mary's High School.

Rita Rupp Donaldson, Hilda,
Lester Rupp, and Vincent Wilberding.

OUR OLD HOUSE 1937

The farmhouse, 1937.

Hilda and Lester fishing.

Hilda and Lester.

Hilda and Joyce at a book signing.

Hilda clowning around on vacation.

Joyce cutting her mother's nails.

Four generations: daughter Lois, granddaughter Kathy holding great-granddaughter Stephanie, and Hilda.

Hilda kicking up her heels with three sisters: Della Broderson, Margy Golden, and Aggie Thomsen.

Hilda's church directory photo.

Hilda at age eighty-three.

During this social expansion, Mom learned to crochet—I still use the first afghan she made—took ceramics classes, went to Tupperware parties, became a "Pink Lady" volunteer serving snacks at the Mental Health Institute and joined in helping with parties at one of the local nursing homes. She remained active in some of the social groups she joined until her death. These included several birthday-luncheon and card clubs, plus a royal rummy group with cousins and other friends. The year before she died, I gave Mom a ride to the Family Table restaurant where she met seven other women, aged seventy-eight to ninety-six. There they were—actively aging—each with their own health issues but happy to be together to enjoy friendship. As I drove away I wondered, "What will I be like if I live that long?" I hoped I'd have that much zest, and the good fortune of long-lasting friendships.

"The hat party" remains one of my fondest memories. Mom was eighty-two that year. I must admit I groaned inwardly when she suggested I join her for a women's brunch where everyone donned a unique hat. This program included prizes given for the most creative and unusual design. I treasure my memory of seeing the look on Mom's face as she took in the gathering. I glanced over to see a charmed expression, like the joyful glow of a child enchanted with a new toy. Every person, bizarre hat, and piece of conversation brought her unmistakable pleasure. How happy I felt to see my mother in that captivating moment when I became more keenly aware of the simplicity and beauty of her joy and how much she loved life.

One aspect of social events that Mom always expressed interest in was the food. Because she grew up during an era when food was scarce, she paid a lot of attention to what she ate. When she wrote in her diary, Mom often described the current weather conditions and what food she served to guests at home or what she ate at some social event. I still have some of her letters. Almost every one contains some detail in it about what type of salad, sandwich, or desert was offered.

At seventy my mother became a more direct teacher of how to live as an older person. That year she adjusted to being a new widow, moved from the farm to a town residence, had both knees replaced, and made a trip to Texas to sell the trailer home of their brief retirement years. She made her way through those changes peacefully, although grief put a damper on her zest for several years. Gradually, Mom joined me on some of my speaking tour trips and that is when I really came to know her. Early in her marriage she and Dad had vacationed in the Midwest, as well as New York City and California. Later on, they made annual trips to Waco, Texas, to visit Mom's favorite sister, Elsie Vassar, and to Fruita, Colorado, where my older brother Jerry and his family lived. But for the most part she traveled very little outside of Iowa. I loved having her along. She accepted every invitation and relished the experience. Her excitement ignited my own. I never tired of my mother's companionship and the enriching conversations we shared.

During those years of travel Mom and I became good friends. Our trips eased her loneliness and fed her thirst for adventure. For at least eight years we journeyed to New England, New York State, Oregon, Washington State, Wisconsin, Illinois, Colorado, Montana, Wyoming, Arkansas, Texas, Missouri, and Hawaii. Certain moments are imprinted on my memory, special ones in which Mom's unassuming delight and open eagerness touched my heart.

Our time in New England remains the most memorable. What sparkling eyes she had when we dined at a quaint restaurant near a Cape Cod shoreline. Later that week she surprised me with her appreciation of beauty when she remarked, "I just love this" as we crossed a picturesque, wooden bridge in the New Hampshire woods. In Vermont, the autumn trees displayed their best colors and she took to saying "Wow!" every time we turned a bend in the road and came across another glorious hillside. Then she got carried away and began greeting the most beautiful views with, "Wow, wow, wow!" Her voice carried such happiness that I joined with her "Wow, wow, wow!" Each time we let out the exclamation, we followed it with a gleeful laugh.

One of our last trips took us to her beloved, ancestral Dyersville, the place that afforded Mom some of her happiest childhood memories. We looked up cousins and visited her old friend, Marcie, now infirm and residing at a care center. Our time in that little Iowa town held a certain poignancy, not only for the memories it brought back to her, but for the unspoken reality that old age would not allow a future return. This is one of the aspects of growing old not always spoken about—the "last time" of seeing someone or being somewhere—situations that speak loudly of forthcoming death but are seldom acknowledged verbally.

On Sunday morning, before we departed for Cherokee, Mom expressed a wish to visit a cousin she'd not communicated with for a long time. We found the address and hoped he would be home as we stood by the front door waiting for an answer to our knock. After several minutes, the door opened a crack. A broad shouldered, stocky man didn't even bother to say "hello." He just said, "Yes?" in a cold voice, obviously not pleased we were there. That didn't faze Mom. She explained, "I'm Hilda Rupp. My husband, Lester, and I used to visit your folks." She then went on to tell him how they were related. The man's demeanor changed completely, and he invited us in for a visit. When we were back in the car Mom chuckled and explained what I missed at the front door. In our Sunday church clothes he undoubtedly took us to be two missionaries, perhaps Jehovah's Witnesses. Yes, my mother could always find humor in something that initially presented discomfort.

Mom not only maintained her gusto for life, she became more open-minded. For a good portion of her life, she held a number of personal and cultural biases. While she did not gossip, and felt uncomfortable when others did, she kept her distance from people whose attitude or way of life contrasted significantly from her own. This was especially true regarding strangers. When their manner of dressing, ethnicity, or skin color differed from hers, she embarrassed me more than once by leaning over and commenting in a stage whisper about someone's color of hair, body size, or style of clothes.

Fortunately, these biased comments lessened with age and an increase of travel. Instead of getting stuck in old ways of thinking and relating, Mom expanded in openness toward diversity. During hospitalization in Sioux City, one of her main nurses, a man from India, spoke with an accent. In past years, she might have simply tolerated his nursing care. This time, she not only genuinely liked this man, she praised his medical skills to her visitors.

This quality of openness continued to manifest itself as Mom grew older. Other innate qualities I admired about her, such as determination, feistiness, generosity, other-centeredness, and kindheartedness ripened. I grew daily in admiration of how my aged mother maintained a passion for life and kept the fire in her spirit alive in spite of a significant amount of physical pain and discomfort. Up to the very end, she entered into and enjoyed life to the utmost. Five years before her death, I went over some questions about aging with Mom. When I asked for advice about growing older, her first response summed it up: "Go with the flow."

That is exactly what she did.

CHAPTER 6

A FIRM FOUNDATION of FAITH

A Firm Foundation

> Soon after birth you were
> lifted from the cradle and
> carried to the baptismal font.
> There you received the gift
> and the burden of a religion
> determined to bless
> and bind you to its moorings.
>
> Perhaps you cried out with
> an innocent babe's alarm
> at the startling wetness
> flowing over your forehead,
> that first gesture birthing you
> into a faith community.
>
> Through the ensuing years
> and into the last phase of life
> you turned with confidence
> to that foundation of strength,
> gave of yourself regardless
> of difference and desire,
> sought comfort and satisfaction,

stayed faithful, remained dutiful
to request and requirement
in hope of what might be received
in return.

And did you receive it?

The current of inner strength,
the flow of courage that outwrestled
the demon of depression
and loss of physical vitality,
the peace with which you moved
toward death, each of these testifies
to that firm foundation begun
when you were lifted from the cradle
and carried into church.

—**Joyce Rupp**

But the best thing we can build for the future
is the structure of our faith. God is the rock
and represents our only real security
in a changing world.

—Emilie Griffin
Souls in Full Sail

Little do we know when we are young what might sustain us as we grow old. What we either take for granted or are unaware of in our youth might well be the very thing that carries us through some of the more difficult aspects of life later on. What is certain is that we will need something foundational on which to rest our response to waning energy and persistent limitation of body, mind, and spirit. This "something" can lessen the tendency toward despondency and self-pity. It can keep us grounded in a positive and peaceful manner. In my mother's case, her religious faith provided this sound underpinning as she grew older.

In her youth, I doubt that Mom paid much attention to how her spiritual beliefs established a foundation for hope and resiliency. Organized religion naturally existed as part of her personal journey, something she expected to travel with throughout life as an inherent companion. She could not have known then what a gift it would be as she turned toward elderhood. More than anything else, this faith sustained and nurtured her durable spirit when she eventually lost most of her physical energy.

My mother entered the Roman Catholic religion when her parents brought her, their infant daughter Hildegard, to be baptized at St. Mary's church in Remsen, Iowa. As she grew into a young woman, this church provided a secure environment for worship, as well as for elementary and secondary education at parish schools nearby. During her forty-nine years of married life she lived a mile and a half from Visitation Church, located by a gravel road in a tiny hamlet named Maryhill. Besides the church, this rural village of mostly German farm families consisted of the pastor's rectory, a three-room elementary school, a convent housing the sisters who taught there, the janitor's home and a little grocery store. All of us children attended school at Maryhill. Our mother dutifully taught us the prayers we were to memorize and made sure we attended church services.

Mom's involvement in the parish community was more than an appendage to her life. She often attended daily Mass, went to novenas and seasonal church activities during Advent and Lent and participated in most of the church's social functions. She took meals to the parish priests and invited them to special celebrations at our home. As a child witnessing my mother's involvement in the parish, I assumed everyone's Catholic mother did this sort of thing. I never questioned how much she helped out in the parish until much later.

Nor did I consider out of the ordinary what my mother did for us children to enable our participation in special church celebrations, like May Crowning and First Communion. In May, she cut the long, white-blossomed stems on the arching bridal-veil spiraea bushes and formed them into garlands to wear in our hair as we processed in the crowning of the statue of Mary with a wreath of flowers. For our First Communion, she sewed special white dresses for us girls, blue suits for the boys, and bought small, laminate-covered prayer books and white rosaries for us to use.

Mom spent untold hours helping with funeral dinners and parish fund-raisers, such as the big "Maryhill dinner." Several times she presided as president of the Women's Guild. This "yes" meant a lot of work. Its central responsibility involved food provision, along with organizing table service for the dinner, which fed between five hundred and one thousand visitors. She also joined the women in baking pies and preparing other food donated to the project. On the night of the event, with no air conditioning in the outdoor pavilion, Mom stood for hours on the concrete floor, sweating profusely in the intense August heat. I remember times of her being exhausted or physically ill, but she insisted on doing her part to contribute to that parish endeavor.

Generosity never trailed far behind my mother's gratitude. Forty years later, I discovered that bigheartedness in another way. I accompanied her when she won big playing the casino machines at Tama, Iowa. When she first found me in another part of the building to tell me about it, she whispered, "Joyce, come with me into the bathroom." She sounded so serious and kind of afraid, as if something dreadful was about to happen to her.

Of course, I immediately thought the worst, given her constant health issues, figuring she must be feeling really ill if she wanted us to go into the restroom. How astonished I was when she opened her purse and showed me the $2,500 she had just won. Her concern was having someone see all that money and try to steal it from her. After joyfully relating her astounding news, Mom followed it with, "I'm going to give ten percent of this to the church." She felt this donation would express her appreciation for the support she received both spiritually and communally from her faith, as well as her thankfulness for the surprise reception of that cash.

In spite of my mother's best efforts to be a good congregant, an alcoholic pastor called her in one day and gave her a devastating, verbal thrashing. She eventually stood up to him and refused to be overpowered by his judgmental harshness. Many people experiencing this kind of treatment would "never have darkened the door of the church again." But not my mother. She wouldn't give up what she found to be of great benefit. The value she placed on her religious faith enabled her to remain a responsible parishoner who continued to graciously participate and help out when needed.

As with a lot of older persons, Mom merged prayer into more and more of her life. Four years before her death, she announced one morning as she entered the kitchen, "I must have gotten through my rosary last night because I had it hanging up when I awoke this morning." Until I heard that remark, I had not an inkling about her evening habit of praying the rosary and then reaching over to hang its worn, red beads on the bedpost before she fell asleep.

Actually, I knew very little of my mother's spiritual life because our personal relationship with the divine lends itself more to mystery than to disclosure. The intimacy regarding one's hidden faith-life tends to keep others from conversation about this part of a person's experience. This secret domain contains a sphere of connection with the Holy One that others rarely have the privilege to enter and, then, only when we vulnerably allow them to do so. Thus, when we companion someone older, the reality of their spiritual life often remains concealed.

That is how I perceive my hesitancy in speaking about faith with my mother. I wanted to respect her personal beliefs. I felt uneasy in inquiring about her relationship with God. Yet, I could see and sense her unbounded trust in the One to whom she prayed by how she went about her spiritual practices and by her resilient approach toward the difficult things that happened to her. I found this trust, too, in her ability to move beyond the discouragement and gloom that enters anyone's inner space from time to time, especially when facing increasing diminishment. She continually turned toward her faith to lead her to joy after sorrow, to relief after pain, to hope after disappointment.

Emilie Griffin refers to the worth of older persons' spirituality in *Souls in Full Sail*:

> Spiritual life—prayer and reflection—can help us develop strength for the later years. Not only do we include a variety of spiritual practices in

our lives; also we develop a deeper relationship with God, one that is not based on duty but on genuine friendship.

For me, the relationship with God is the chief love story of my life. And it is always an adventure, often a matter of changing course and finding new ways forward, new beginnings. We are shy about speaking of our love of God in such romantic terms. We speak of "the spiritual life" or "the life of prayer."[1]

I'll never know if my mother's relationship with the Holy One bore a similarity to the love story Griffin describes, but there are definite signs indicating Mom's belief in the value of prayer. One of the treasures we discovered after her death included a small prayer book, titled *Family Prayer*, which we found in the bathroom. Its yellowed pages, thin and edged with use, include a dog-eared one containing the prayer "Mother Mary." This entreaty to the mother of Jesus asks Mary: "Be a protecting Mother to my children. Guard their bodies and keep them in health and strength. Guard their minds and keep them pure and strong and happy in the love of God. Always Mother, protect them and keep them under your motherly care."

A chance remark volunteered by Mom let me in on this aspect of her inner life. She mentioned praying for each of us children as she rode her stationary bike. She hated exercise and this probably provided a method of distraction. She could have chosen some other non-spiritual diversion so her comment told me not only that she prayed for us but that she integrated prayer into her daily activities. When I asked Mom what she prayed during that time, she replied, "I pray the rosary, a decade for each one of you kids, and now I am praying one for Lois and her new job." That revelation truly touched me. As a woman with a lot of health issues causing daily pain and limited activity, Mom focused on those she loved, rather than on herself. This was typical of our mother's generous spirit.

As Mom's years dwindled, one way this generosity continued to grow was through her prayer life. Mom liked to "do" little kindnesses for others. When her health waned, praying for people gave her a way to continue to do be kind. Her spiritual practice taught me that when elderly people become less physically active and unable to accomplish "good deeds," they continue to contribute significantly to the well-being of others through the gift of prayer. How I long for more senior persons to realize the power of their prayerful presence.

I owe it to my mother's prayer ministry that I remained a member of my religious community when I seriously considered leaving it as I approached my fiftieth birthday, an unsettled year for me. When I pondered my choices and decisions, I decided to talk with Mom about it. In explaining my dilemma, I thought she might urge me to keep my commitment. Instead, she did not nudge me to stay or to leave. She simply suggested, "Why don't you think about it some more?" and then added, "I'll pray for you." In that moment I felt such tremendous support from her love and faith.

Mom remained faithful to Roman Catholicism throughout her life, but that does not mean she easily followed certain church precepts. In her late seventies, she confided how difficult she found the law preventing her from practicing birth control during her child-bearing years. After six children, she visited the local pastor to seek approval to have her fallopian tubes tied, but he disapproved and gave an adamant "No." As much as she loved the eight of us children, Mom wished she could have chosen how many she birthed, and when. She told me one day, "I just learned to accept what was." Like her own mother, she lived many a day as an exhausted, weary woman.

After two miscarriages in her thirties, Mom birthed a seventh and an eighth child and then had another miscarriage. With this one so much bleeding ensued that she wore thick bath towels to absorb the blood while Dad drove her to the hospital. How frightened she must have been, remembering how her mother hemorrhaged to death. After this miscarriage, her physician warned her, "Hilda, you absolutely cannot have any more pregnancies," and urged her to have a hysterectomy. Even so, she first went to her parish priest to receive permission before going through with the surgery.

This need to request Church approval reappeared at age eighty. Because my mother rarely spoke about her personal experience of faith, she surprised me by initiating a conversation regarding her reception of the Sacrament of Reconciliation (formerly known as "Confession") at an Advent prayer service. As she disclosed the content of that experience, relief filled her voice. "There was this wonderful young priest. I told him, 'I don't go to confession as often as I used to. Now that I'm older I really don't commit a lot of sins. I'm not sure what to say or why I'm here.'" She went on to describe how good she felt afterward because he not only listened to her, he responded with, "It's okay, Hilda. You only have to go once a year. Devote your life to helping others and doing good." (If she had been physically able, I think she might have danced a jig after telling me about that liberating moment.)

Mom also managed to find humor in ludicrous religious situations. She liked to tell of a certain summer fishing trip in Canada. The Protestant couple who joined my parents for that excursion also went along with them on the sixty-mile round trip from their cabin to attend a Saturday evening Mass in a small village. Upon arrival, they discovered they were the only four persons there. In spite of their age (all in their late sixties) the retired, stooped-shouldered priest focused on the topic of birth control for his homily. Mom laughed as she spoke, "He kept emphasizing the church's position and how we were not to use it. Imagine, at our age!"

While my mother was not overly pious, she did practice certain personal devotions. Candles burned for only two occasions in our home—"to have God's protection from bad weather" and to celebrate birthdays. We didn't need a meteorologist on the farm to tell us about the threat of severe storms. All we had to do was look and see the candle

Mom lit when the sky darkened and the humid, windy air changed to an ominous silence.

Another devotion consisted of praying to St. Anthony to help find lost objects. She professed great trust in this practice. One time, during a phone conversation, I described my frustration at not being able to find three music CDs I had purchased a week earlier. I'd called the store where I purchased them, combed my office, looked everywhere in the car, to no avail. Mom immediately asked, "Have you prayed to St. Anthony?"

"No, I didn't think of that," I replied, knowing she couldn't see me roll my eyes. But when I hung up the phone, I thought, "Oh well, it won't hurt to look once more" even though I had searched my car thoroughly at least a half dozen times. Lo and behold, within ten minutes I held all three CDs in my hand after locating them where they had become stuck in the springs underneath the car seat. When I called to tell Mom, I heard her jubilant, "See, I told you so."

Although my mother never acted self-righteous about her religion, at the same time, she adhered faithfully to its rules. In her mid-seventies I noticed somewhat of a change. She began questioning certain precepts and seemed to be less wedded to them. Attending Mass on the weekend was an absolute must for her, but as her body weakened she did not fret if she felt too disabled or unwell to do so. Someone else in her situation might have pushed on to follow the law of necessary attendance, or feel guilty about not going. She didn't lose her desire to be there, but she simply accepted the situation. She watched the Mass broadcast on television and gratefully welcomed reception of Holy Communion when my brother-in-law Jim, a Eucharistic minister, brought this to her on Sunday mornings.

At eighty, Mom felt freer to express what she was thinking in regard to the Church. She turned to me one day and queried, "Don't you think it's about time this pope retires?" (referring to John Paul II). I was amazed she could differ with a church tradition and suggest it needed changing. Another time she announced, "I think eventually it's not going to make any difference which religion you have, as long as you're a good person." That unexpected statement indicated her developing open-mindedness and freedom. Here was my aging mother, ever faithful and solid in her own religion, equally content with someone belonging to another. How much she had grown since the time when Roman Catholic law forbade her to attend a non-Catholic service.

As Mom grew older, I kept hearing new things from her in regard to her personal faith and religious beliefs. But just about the time I thought she might be moving off center and going a bit toward "the left" she'd prove otherwise. Several years before her death, when I called her on Ash Wednesday, she mentioned abstaining from meat that day. I questioned her doing this and insisted that someone her age did not have to adhere to this church law. Her voice grew tight as she expressed disagreement, "Oh yes, we do!" I let that one go, but I did a little research. Sure enough, she was right about the age thing. Still, with all her health problems there was little doubt she could have foregone the no-meat day. But not Hilda Rupp.

My mother also developed some new religious observances. Not washing clothes on Sunday was one of these. This decision must have come from a conversation with friends or something she read or heard about on television.

Mom was never a preachy sort of person. She acted on her religious beliefs but did not shove them onto others. She enjoyed hearing and telling an off-color joke and certainly wasn't a prude about sex. That's why I was quite surprised about another late-in-life occurrence. Aunt Rita gave Mom romance novels to read. One day I noticed she crossed out all the four-letter "F-words" in those books. When I asked her about this, she got rather stormy, telling me how she hated that word.

These varied changes in religious practices and beliefs ought not to have surprised me as much as they did. They led me to ask why it is that we who are younger presume it's okay for us to continually grow and change and, yet, do not expect or perhaps even want this from our elders. What is it about us that leads to our astonishment or concern when they begin to think or act differently? Surely they have every right to change as much as we do when an awareness draws them toward another direction. Why do we hesitate to accept our elders' approach to thinking or living in a different way from the past? Is it because these changes impinge on our comfort level and ask that we let go of how we've known them?

While my mother kept an open mind and heart and became more adaptable about certain aspects of her faith, she stood strongly on her moral convictions. Being a faith-filled person, Mom did her best to live a virtuous life. I never experienced her living anything other than an exemplary moral life. That is why she felt especially pained about an incident that left her feeling, as she put it, "disgusted and upset."

This occurrence took place not long after Dad died. Mom got an opportunity to practice her ethical convictions when the doorbell rang, and she discovered an old friend of theirs on the doorstep. After this man's wife died, he had remarried a few years later. My parents considered this couple good friends and occasionally joined in social events with the two of them. Mom thought this friend had come to pay a visit of condolence. She soon discovered that his purpose in visiting focused mainly on having sex with her. How quickly this man learned of her high moral standards as she abruptly showed him to the door and warned angrily, "Don't ever come back again!"

After that disturbing visit, I wonder if the memory of an incident in her early twenties came to mind. Her solid morality met a challenge when she worked a month or so as a cook in a boarding room house, feeding seven or eight men each day. The owner, a bachelor, kept pursuing her with lewd advances. Each night she locked her door in hope of being safe. In the morning, this man (who couldn't remember Mom's real name), came to her room, banged on the door and shouted, "Hilary! Hilary! It's time to get up." How fearful she felt when he hung around the house, ogling her. Yet, her strength of character helped her manage the situation without harm coming to herself.

My mother's desire to be a God-centered woman deepened and strengthened her resilient spirit and personal integrity. I look at her life from this view and I see why she continued to engage in a religion that did not always serve her well. But it served her well enough. The basic tenets of Roman Catholicism that Mom chose to live by enabled her not only to endure the more difficult things of life, but to also become a woman of solid ethical standards with a spirit of generosity and loving kindness.

CHAPTER 7

THE BEST *Friend* I EVER HAD

At the Front Door

A fresh arrival of friendship,
unexpected upon reaching
seventy, the heart well-calloused
from life's adversity,

the voice of awakening
possibility stands there
with enthusiasm,
waiting to be welcomed.

Sheer joy, long lain idle
amid tarnished energy
and the body's decision
to limp along instead of run,
rubs her sleepy eyes
in blinking amazement.

An invitation to step out,
to go beyond
where the past limited
the view, to break down
the door nailed shut
by angry demand and loud opinion.

Finally, in these remaining years
a friend so fine, so good, so true,
so full of dancing spirit
that all the hard years slip away
with barely a whisper.

—**Joyce Rupp**

Each friend represents a world in us,
a world possibly not born until they arrive,
and it is only by this meeting that a new world is born.

—Anaïs Nin
The Diary of Anaïs Nin

A fresh friendship in my mother's seventieth year taught me
we are never too old to enter into a vibrant, life-changing
relationship. I watched with gratitude as Mom slowly grew
beyond her grief over Dad's death and began sprouting
wings of joy and freedom, wings that took her to inner and
outer places long submerged in never-ending work and the
voice of my father's demanding expectations.

In spite of what Mom experienced with Dad's patriarchy,
she felt acute grief after his death. Several months after
his passing, she made a decision to move from the family
farm to a condominium in the nearby town of Cherokee.
At seventy, Mom knew her developing health issues would
be best tended if she lived closer to medical assistance.
She recognized a growing inability to be alone in the less
populated countryside. In addition, her always generous
spirit wanted Roger and Opal (my brother and sister-in-
law, who worked the farm) to live in the family home. She
stepped away with courage from the place where she had
lived and loved for forty-nine years, a place that contained
a good portion of her personal history. Life there not only
required an immense amount of daily toil, it also held
bountiful love.

As Mom prepared to leave the farm, her resilient spirit enabled her to face with quiet acceptance what lay ahead rather than dwell on what she was leaving behind, especially the house built during my tenth year. How well I remember her excitement and joy when we finally moved from our drab, hundred-year-old home into our sparkling new one. Back then Mom's happiness and pride showed in how spotlessly clean she kept the house.

I noticed the freedom and simplicity with which she sorted and packed what she would take with her as she left her home. I did not realize then that the desire to live more simply often stirs strongly in those who reach their senior years. Once Mom left the farmhouse with so many memories, she tried not to look back. This life event, like so many others, asked her to yield to the inevitable as it thrust her forward. She gave herself to that requirement of surrender as fully as she could, although it presented a challenge from time to time. After one of her visits to the home-place Mom divulged her ongoing desire to have things there remain as she had once kept them: "I keep telling myself it's not mine anymore, and once you give it away you have to let go of it and let it be." Even though this desire tugged at her heart, she did not give in to the impulse to try to change things but continued to move on from what had been.

The way Mom departed the family homestead taught me another lesson, this one about the value of letting go. The hidden secret of surrendering to the inevitable is that it often contains mysteries of which we know little until we live into them. What a surprise awaited my mother once she bade farewell to her home of forty-nine years. The condominium to which Mom moved connected on the north side to Wilda Munson's place. The two women had met briefly in previous years but had never established a friendship. After Mom settled in, it did not take long for them to discover that destiny intended them to develop a special relationship. This alliance came alive when Mom finally received a total knee replacement after a few months in her fresh residence. While Mom was recovering from this surgery and somewhat incapacitated, Wilda began stopping over to keep her company. She would walk over with something freshly baked, knock on the unlocked door, open it and call in, "Hilda, are you ready for a visitor?" The answer always came back, "Sure, c'mon in!"

Lo and behold, within a few months Wilda and my mother became best of friends. *Hilda and Wilda.* They were quite the pair. They even looked a bit like one another, both being of hefty, short build. Each was about the same age and dressed in colorful polyester pantsuits. They both had a zest for life. Mom's spirit waited like a fledgling bird prepared to take off, ready for someone to cheer her on. I watched as Wilda's effervescent spirit awakened this sense of adventure in my grieving mother, and as my mother provided a kindhearted presence for Wilda, whose debilitated husband languished in a nursing home. Each woman carried her own particular sadness, and this new friendship eased those hurts.

At the time their friendship stirred, Mom's and Wilda's lives were approaching the reality described by Henry Simmons and Jane Wilson in *Soulful Aging*: "Most of us, after we are seventy-five, experience increasing loneliness. Friends die; others become housebound or find traveling difficult. People find us less interesting, and so friends come to see us less frequently. This makes life less interesting and exciting. There may be a deeper loneliness that we find difficult to communicate. We know that very soon we shall have no part in this world, and so it becomes very precious."[1]

Wilda turned out to be the best thing that could have happened to my mother at that particular time. Not long after Mom recovered her ability to walk, Wilda whisked her off on the first of many "mystery tours"—taking her to museums, to overnights at Bed and Breakfasts, stage plays and musical performances, experiences her new friend, Hilda, had been unable to attend until then. After awhile, Mom began plotting her own mystery excursions to take Wilda on. These two absolutely relished surprising and energizing each other. One of the two would knock on the other's door and announce, "Okay, get your purse. We're taking off!" and away they would go for a delightful escapade.

Mom's new friendship enlivened numerous innate inclinations that had grown quiet in her. One of these involved taking exciting risks. I knew from stories I heard of my mother's youth that she had been a risk-taker. On one occasion Mom and her good friend and first cousin

Martha hitchhiked as teenagers to Sioux City, thirty-six miles away. Two truckers stopped, gave them a ride, took them out for dinner and brought them back home to Remsen. Fortunately, this situation took place in an era when young women could do that sort of thing without serious consequences. Still, it was a considerable risk and took an adventurous spirit to consider traveling that way.

Occasionally, the adventures of Wilda and Hilda worried me. Hearing of how the two of them traipsed around the town one winter night to see the Christmas lights and their car nearly slipping over the edge of a steep, icy hill left me feeling uneasy. Knowing they temporarily lost their way while exploring back country roads on their way to an Iowa casino caused me to be concerned. If they ended up with car trouble neither one of them had legs strong enough to walk for help (cell phones did not exist then). Yet, I knew what they chose to do kept their spirits vibrant and healthy so I tried not to chide Mom—as adult children tend to do when they are anxious about their aging parents' well-being.

Wilda awakened so much in Mom's life. I had no idea how much my mother enjoyed symphonies, films, art exhibits, and theater productions until Wilda invited her to those events. During this time Mom began using her most-beloved slogan, "Fly while you still have wings." Wilda helped those wings to unfold, wings clipped for far too many years by a life of raising eight children and a husband who kept her in a patriarchal straightjacket.

Gradually I became aware of my mother having fun for the pure sake of it. I heard more contentment and joy in Mom's voice during her years with Wilda than at any other time. For a change, she didn't have to work, as she used to do on fishing trips with Dad. In the past, the opportunities that presented themselves for that kind of relaxing play were rare. When Wilda showed up in Mom's life she was ready for wider possibilities, and her adventurous friend provided them.

Their friendship included more than leisurely quests. Equally valuable was Wilda's solid commitment to spiritual growth and prayer. Although Mom, a cradle Catholic, knew friends from other religious denominations, she rarely took part in their worship services or devotions. Wilda invited her to participate in a Methodist scripture study, something which brought Mom significant inspiration, but Wilda's spiritual influence did not end there.

One weekend when I visited Mom, we sat down to lunch, just the two of us. I expected her usual "You say the prayer, Joyce." Instead, I heard a voice other than mine praying aloud, not the rote Catholic prayer "Bless us, O Lord," but a creative one. *My mother was praying aloud in her own words*—I felt utter astonishment. Where did she learn this way of praying and find the vulnerability to do so? Why, from Wilda, of course.

From this close friend Mom also gained the ability to name and talk about her emotional world. Of all the gifts my mother received from Wilda, this may have been the best one. Being able to vocalize interior responses to life's ups and downs provides release and support for anyone, particularly for older persons whose aging process often isolates them mentally and emotionally from those who've not yet lived that many years. In the past, Mom's life always included women friends with whom she found companionship, understanding, and enjoyment, but Wilda conveyed something more. She brought her humble vulnerability to Mom. This friend spoke openly with her about what caused distress and sorrow. When Wilda voiced her struggles to Mom, she often cried. This openness allowed my mother to be increasingly unguarded and to more readily reveal her deeper self as well.

How I wish I could have heard those conversations. After this friend died, Mom said of her, "I could fill a whole notebook about Wilda." What I do know of their intimate exchanges came mostly from what Mom chose to tell me and from my observations of their at-home-ness with each other. Once in a while I happened to be with them at the kitchen table where I was fortunate to hear their comforting and engaging exchanges.

What trust these two women established in that loving relationship. Their friendship not only took the edge off of their loneliness, it brought out the best part of themselves. Theirs was the kind of relationship Joan Chittister describes in *The Friendship of Women*: "Friendship is the process of opening ourselves to the care, to the wisdom, of the other. The love of friendship is the love that holds no secrets, has no unasked questions, no unspoken thoughts, no unanswered concerns. Friendship extends us into places we have not gone before and cannot go alone."[2]

The bond between Mom and Wilda increased in their later years because both risked opening their minds and hearts. They accepted each other without judgment and never considered themselves too old to be enriched and stretched by the other's insights and way of approaching life. When I was with these two friends, I did not hear either of them gossip or bemoan "how awful the world is." Both looked for the good in one another and in the larger world and found it.

These two senior women lived with grateful, faith-filled hearts and became the better for it. Their unexpected bond reminded me that we do not know when another person may come and awaken dormant dreams in us. There is always something more to be discovered about our deeper self, always additional features to be drawn forth, celebrated and shared. Hilda and Wilda's openness to friendship with one another taught me to never shut the door on possibility, no matter what age I might be.

Six years after this late-in-life friendship birthed, Wilda developed cervical cancer and succumbed after a year's treatment. Toward the end of her life, Wilda expressed her reluctance about dying to Mom: "I'm afraid of how much my death will hurt you, Hilda." After they had an honest talk about this, Mom found the courage to assure her dear friend, "I'll be okay. I will really miss you but I want you to be at peace." Without realizing it, at that moment Mom returned the gift of freedom Wilda had given to her. It was a different sort of freedom, a much needed one that helped her dear friend transition peacefully when the time of death arrived.

Wilda was a rare jewel. No other friend matched the expansiveness she brought to Mom's wings. Her death left a huge gap in my mother's heart and life. After the funeral Mom turned to me and said with such sorrow, "I think she was the best friend I ever had."

Mom turned seventy-seven the year Wilda died. She lived seven more years. After this friend's death, I noticed the quiet loneliness elderly people experience begin to seep into my mother's spirit more forcefully. In the following years, Mom occasionally commented, "All my friends are gone." I slowly began to understand the depth of an older person's silent isolation when most of their generation disappears, leaving the surviving elder unable to communicate adequately with others who do not carry their shared remembrances.

Friend after friend of Mom's kept passing away. When she was seventy-eight, her diary included a list of twenty names and the dates of their deaths that year. With each one who died after Wilda, there was one less person in her life who understood what it was like to be her age, one less person who shared her history of social and cultural memories. This progression of loss moved her quietly toward thoughts of her own future death. One day Mom told me about a tough angina attack the week before. She said "I just took my pills." And then added emphatically, "I'm *not* going to the hospital."

Knowing how distraught she felt, I didn't blame her for being so adamant. I thought, "Aging is, in many ways, the pits, no matter how good an attitude one has." Much of the sadness and discouragement ends up being swallowed rather than communicated with those who are healthier and younger.

A few months before that angina attack, Mom called to tell me in a flat voice that her good friend, Margaret George, had died. I grew concerned about the lack of sadness in Mom's voice. She and Margaret's friendship went way back to their youth. It did not occur to me then that the heart can only respond to so much. Years later, I comprehended this fact better when an eighty-year-old friend of mine explained her absence at a funeral, "Ten friends in a year died. I can't go to any more funerals for awhile." I then understood that if older people let in all the sadness from these deaths that the emotional overload could consume them.

In her poem *The Gardener*, Mary Oliver asks the soul-searching question "Have I endured loneliness with grace?"[3] If my mother had responded to that question at the end of her life, she could have done so positively. She withstood this unwanted portion of her life with dignity and acceptance, but there is little doubt Mom felt lonely. She loved being around others and longed for company. Yet, she never whined or complained about the lack of people to fill her life. Self-pity did not enter in to lessen her core resiliency nor did it leap out to cause others to feel guilty.

Instead, I noticed how Mom took on the practice of ending every phone call received with "Thank you for calling," indicating gratitude for a person to talk with and help her forget for a while the ache that never fully went away. Or she would muse about something that hinted of loneliness beneath it, like the time she commented about my older sister, "I wish Lois wasn't so busy. She works too hard." As a mother, she had genuine concern for her daughter, but I also believe the comment indicated, "Oh, how I wish she had more time for me."

The closest Mom came to lamenting her lonesomeness came in her farewells. I knew she didn't want me to go. I felt her sadness, as well as my own, when she expressed her reluctance at my departures with "I wish you could stay longer," or "I love it when you come to visit me. Hurry and come back soon," or, "I loved having you here." Because Mom found it difficult to express her deeper feelings, I recognized the love and intensity in those comments. During the last five years, her hugs of hello and goodbye grew in strength, making departure increasingly difficult.

The year before her death I could see tears film her eyes when she hugged me one more time and said, "I love you lots" with—heavy emphasis on "lots." The tenderness in her voice nearly crashed in on me. I hated to go. I knew she'd have a tough day, especially with no plans for it. But I had to go on with life and she did too. I called her when I arrived home and when I voiced my concern about leaving her, she assured me, "I'm okay. I'll write letters this afternoon."

Even when Mom's body became weaker those beautiful embraces continued to wrap around those who visited, a reminder not only of her fondness for us but the need of elders for physical touch—whether that be a hug, a touch on the arm, holding a hand, or a kiss on the cheek. I looked forward to Mom's hugs and recognized in them how much she yearned for a sense of belonging and connectedness amid her growing sense of emotional isolation. I also knew that no matter how long I stayed, I could not eliminate all the loneliness stored inside of her.

Sundays proved to be the toughest days. Mom never said, "I'm lonely" or "Why don't you call more often?" She would just get through it, try to busy herself, make some phone calls, work another crossword puzzle. As I became more cognizant of this loneliness, I called each Sunday during the last year of her life, yet nothing could erase the reality that more and more of her friends and those she related to with ease were no longer there for her.

Loneliness never departed completely once Wilda left Mom's life. Without realizing it, Mom spoke more and more often about the emptiness she felt because of the loss of her friends. Six months before her death she again indicated loneliness by simply stating, "I have no close friends left." This occurred during a conversation in which she tried to tell me why she was ready for her own death. I asked her what it was like to have all these loved ones gone. She paused and then responded, "I guess I feel lost." While it pained me to hear that response, I also knew this to be the inevitable consequence of out-living the significant persons in one's life.

Not even the strongest amount of resilience could keep loneliness from occupying a permanent place in my mother's heart. Yet the memory of the best friend she ever had remained as a precious gift of comfort and strength. This surprising friendship served to keep Mom resiliently leaning into what remained to be enjoyed in her life—even when increasing physical diminishment threatened to steal that enjoyment from her.

CHAPTER 8

When A NEW DISABILITY *Arrives*

Concerning My Mother's Illness

I pray to be held
together—
or maybe just held—
while the pieces fall,
limp leaves floating
faltering, plummeting,
touched by the silent
raindrops of early Autumn.

I pray to be freed
from the snorting breath
of depression, too close
these past days as it
hovers over my mother's life
with gloomy threats
and the snickering insinuation
of demise.

I pray to let go or to fight,
whichever is necessary,
whatever is best for my mother,

to be with the unspoken pain
of her emotional turning,
some sort of staccato tempo
in aging and transformation,
a dance I've never known before,
not like this in my resilient mother,

and I am unable to learn the movements.

I pray to lighten up,
to observe the free-fall
of weakened confidence
in the loose strands of aging,
to be in this uncertainty
with the acceptance
and patience of a daughter
who loves with a full heart.

—**Joyce Rupp**

When a new disability arrives I look about to see if
death has come, and I call quietly, "Death, is that you?
Are you there?" So far the disability has answered,
"Don't be silly, it's me."
—Florida Scott-Maxwell
The Measure of My Days

The memory of taking my mother to visit her long-time
friend Opal Rupp sticks in my memory like super glue.
Our families shared many festivities and holidays together,
with each of the two mothers capable and efficient in
handling our large families for meals and other activities.
How different these two once-vibrant friends were now as
they sat across from each other in Opal's living room. Now
Opal could only breathe with the help of oxygen and move
around her house with a walker. My mother, who was
recovering from her first heart attack, still could not drive
and continued to sleep long hours due to intense fatigue.
At one point in the conversation, Mom mused sadly to
Opal, "Our carefree days are over." Opal replied in a soft
voice, "At least mine are." I hurt for each of them, seeing
how much each had changed due to increasing physical
disability.

Every new biological limitation challenged my mother's
resiliency. With each change she initially refused to accept
the consequences of the impairing development, believing
she could continue to manage everything as she always
had, counting on her earlier experiences of coping with
unwanted adversity. This desire to remain her energetic

self kept crying out while her physical body repeatedly sent messages to the contrary. No matter how hard she tried, Mom could not generate her former robust self. She went through quite a struggle before entering into a gentle peace regarding the waning of her active life.

After three miscarriages and the ensuing hysterectomy in her early forties, other bodily difficulties slowly accumulated after Mom's fiftieth year. Arthritis had already established itself as a "biggie." Then diabetes followed. Further medical conditions that developed over the next two decades led to more changes—hearing loss, two knee replacements, spinal disc degeneration, implantation of a pace-maker, several heart attacks, frequent bouts of severe bronchitis and pneumonia, congestive heart failure, and diabetic neuropathy.

My mother avoided talking about these medical problems. Perhaps she, like other people in their senior years, feared being thought of and looked upon as "old." Whatever the reason, Mom either hid those discomforts or ignored much of her pain. So I didn't pay a lot of attention to how those illnesses affected her until they became quite obvious.

My first awareness of her physical impairments came after Dad died. Mom and I were in Hawaii walking side by side in a heavy rain and her left foot kept splashing water onto my right shoe. I found this increasingly irritating. Finally I turned and barked, "Stop it, Mom!" She apologized profusely and explained that sometimes her ankle "wouldn't cooperate." I had no idea what neuropathy was or that this side effect of diabetes led to the numbness in her ankle which caused her foot to drag.

I was equally unaware of what it must be like to have body parts resist movement and to have seldom-alleviated, aching pain. I didn't know how Mom sat on the side of her bed in the morning and urged her stiff arthritic bones to cooperate with her need to move. Only after a hot shower could she manage to dress and get around more easily. I discovered this bodily limitation on one of the few occasions my mother ever spoke sharply to me as an adult.

This occurred while we were sitting in her living room and I told her, with a big grin on my face, about being at a convent of my community members. I thought it quite humorous when I walked past a certain sister's bedroom and glanced through a wide-open door to see her sitting naked on the side of the bed. "There she was, Mom, sitting on the edge of her bed, stark naked. Just sitting there like she was waiting for something." It was the fact that this sister kept the door open and was naked in front of everyone that, for some reason, I found comical. To my surprise Mom snapped at me, "That's not funny. You have no idea how hard it is to get out of bed in the morning."

No, I had no idea at all. That reprimand stunned me. She then proceeded to tell me how stiff her body felt when she awakened and how much time it took to get into a hot shower where she encouraged her limbs to move more freely. I quickly realized how insensitive and uncompassionate my little tale sounded. Mom's response humbled and shocked me into seeing the reality of her physical condition. My ignorance could no longer be an excuse.

The most challenging aspect of my mother's aging came about when a harsh depression overtook her following a heart attack that left her body and spirit limp. After spending several days at the hospital with Mom, I left for two weeks in Maine. I knew the seriousness of her heart attack and felt anxious about being that far away, especially since she would be returning home to take care of herself. When I called to check on Mom after the hospital discharged her, I heard a barely audible voice at the other end of the line.

"Mom? Is that you?"

"Yes," came the faint reply.

"What's happening? Are you okay?"

Another pause, and then a whispered, "No. I feel terrible."

Was that my mother? My cheerful, able-to-bounce-back mother? She sounded fragile. Was she dying? Did I need to rush back to Iowa? Never having heard this kind of response from her, I felt extremely distraught, unaware that a side effect of heart medication can include depression. It also took a while for me to comprehend how an accumulation of physical diminishment relentlessly punched her resiliency until it finally retreated to a shadowy place. Thus it was that my mother's buoyant spirit grew weak and her steady enthusiasm fled. Any effort on her part to put up a good front about being strong disappeared.

She certainly knew about depression in the past, but those episodes lasted just a day or two. Mom rarely admitted to feeling downhearted, but every once in a while she alluded to "feeling low." One of these times occurred two years earlier when she began experiencing her body's failure to cooperate. I phoned to ask about her day and she said, "It's been a long afternoon." I inquired further and learned that one of her toes developed an infection that caused her foot to be swollen and sore. She wanted to go to a wedding the next day but couldn't get her shoes on. To make matters worse, her go-to-wedding clothes didn't fit due to the extra body fluid that continually plagued her. She concluded this description of her situation with, "I'm just a fat slob." I felt so bad for her.

Mom recovered from this particular misery in the following days, but recouping her zest for life after the heart attack turned out to be a much lengthier process. When I visited after my return from Maine, I found a mother who no longer wanted to cook, paid no attention to what needed cleaning, and cared not an iota about much of anything. The huge stack of unopened mail by her easy chair confirmed depression's strength.

Where was the mother who loved correspondence, who faithfully remembered every special occasion of friends and family? Where was the durable woman who managed whatever needed to be done, whose cheerful nature uplifted others? She had slipped away. I looked for my mother but found in her place someone I barely recognized.

That depression frightened me. I feared my mother would never get over it, that I'd never have her back again.

To a certain extent that fear was validated. Although Mom eventually recovered from the depression she never returned to her former vitality. The heart attack thrust her into a major transition, from an active, can-do mode to a much more dubious and unsure state of reduced personal vigor.

In *Coming to Age*, author Jane Prétat refers to "late-life transformation" and suggests a number of ways the aging person in transition might respond:

> Times of transition are times of testing. This seems particularly true in the croning years when alternations in our bodies, our psyches and our circumstances repeatedly challenge us. The world around us is altered as old settings vanish to make way for new, old friends depart or become strangers, and familiar roles fall away to leave us naked and exposed. New patterns, new mores and new tasks make it more difficult to recognize ourselves.
>
> When these events occur, we may try to cope in one of several ways. We may retreat in fear from upheaval in our lives, feeling disoriented and out of control. We may armor ourselves for battle and try to destroy our suffering. We may deny that anything is happening to us. Or we may sink into depression and be unable to do much more than get out of bed.[1]

That last option happened to Mom. In her exhausted state, she could accomplish little. For months about all she could manage was to get out of bed. Her days followed an agenda opposite to the one she normally kept. Now there was *no* agenda. No cooking or cleaning, no reading much of anything—not even her prized daily newspaper—and she rarely left the house. She slept until late in the morning and took frequent naps. Instead of voicing frustration and discouragement over the changed way she lived, Mom simply referred to the lack of her former self by summarizing her condition with, "I'm just lazy."

How often I heard her refer to herself in this way as she tried to enter into the adjustments. My mother blamed herself, not her body's limitations, for the way she felt. Undoubtedly this surfaced as a throw-back to her old sense of unworthiness, as well as her belief that she could weather any storm. She failed to see how each illness and hospitalization chipped away more of her valued physical power and emptied her spirit of energy. Finally, the accumulated loss became too great, pushing her to lose an identity that carried and sustained her purpose in life for almost eighty years. No wonder grief entered in full-force.

In the coming months, I noticed that Mom's mental and emotional responses were similar to those associated with grief, including anger, sadness, apathy, fatigue, disinterest, and a lack of focus and concentration. Francis Weller explains, "When we send our grief into exile, we simultaneously condemn our lives to an absence of joy."[2] That is what occurred in the loss of my mother's once-joyful life. She did not recognize the accumulation of grief due to the disappearance of her active self. Thus, she inadvertently "exiled" grief and this left her in an even bleaker, more depressed state, blaming herself instead of her illness for how she felt.

Unattended anger lies beneath depression. How natural for this emotion to arise as a response to adverse physical changes that bring a shift in personal identity. Mom's physical energy lurched into neutral after the heart attack. No wonder anger simmered. One day she initiated a conversation about people living to be a hundred years old by questioning with an irritated tone, "Why do they keep trying to get people to live longer?" Then she asked me what I thought of Dr. Jack Kevorkian, the physician who euthanized elderly patients. She thought his doing so might be okay. I wondered later if this conversation arose from a possible disappointment in not dying from a heart attack, or maybe because she feared becoming even more incapacitated.

Oftentimes a gift lies hidden in what we resist or resent. When she was in her eighties, Florida Scott-Maxwell named this gift of her aging process as that of personal transformation: "We suffer as we change, that life may change in us."[3] This is what Mom's depression offered to her. Because she had so little energy and remained homebound for months, that low-energy time served as a catalyst for coming to terms with a changed identity.

Kathleen Dowling Singh explains how this happens in *The Grace of Dying.* While she writes of those nearing death, her remarks equally apply to those experiencing the limitations of aging and illness.

. . . The person acquiesces to the expanding power of the physical disablements that subtly increase separation from the life he or she has always known. Initially, this enforced withdrawal or isolation causes great psychological and emotional suffering. One experiences one's self as removed from the world of the living, the world of mundane things. When this removal is not our choice . . . there are elements of anger and sadness and surprisingly sharp jealousy, even for those who never thought of themselves as begrudging people. We feel a nostalgic and deep longing for return to the life we once knew as well as the very difficult emotions of self-pity, abandonment, and hopelessness. [4]

My mother never indicated jealousy or self-pity, but she certainly felt hopeless and wanted her old, zest-filled self back. Her response to an absence of useful activity is not that unusual. Like many in Western society, she measured her worth by how much she did. As Jan Chozen Bays writes in *How to Train a Wild Elephant*, "Many of us have a mind that measures self-worth in terms of productivity. If I did not produce anything today, if I did not write a book, give a speech, bake bread, earn money, sell something, buy something, get a good grade on a test, or find my soul mate, then my day was wasted and I am a failure. We give ourselves no credit for taking 'being' time, for just being present."[5]

During her depression the mother I knew lost a good portion of her identity as a productive individual, someone who could always find something to *do* that gave her a sense of purpose and worth. Now she viewed herself as useless. Because she could do so little, she felt she had small value. I sensed this when I offered a compliment or did something for her. She fended off the affirmation or the deed by saying, "I don't deserve that." Usually, I just smiled lovingly and replied, "You're worth it, Mom." In response, she then gave me a look that implied, "You don't know what you're talking about."

How keenly she felt this loss of vigor. One day she acknowledged her feelings about this when we spoke about her depression, "It's true. Older people feel unwanted and useless."

Even after the depression lifted, it took quite a while before Mom accepted that she could be loved and appreciated for herself, that she did not have to "do something" to merit worthiness.

Mom's low energy and downheartedness not only affected her personal identity, it also altered her social life. About five months after the heart attack, Mom still retained an oxygen tank to aid her breathing. That year was the first time she did not join our extended family in gathering for a holiday dinner on Christmas day.

I wrote in my journal the following morning:

> Sometimes Mom seems to be better in spirit. Yet when she is really honest, like last night, she admitted, "I don't care. I just want to do nothing.

I sit in my chair for ten minutes and tell myself I need to get up." I explained how it's her heart, working overly hard, supplying less oxygen. I suggested she will have to adapt her lifestyle. I think she hears me. It's tough. When I kissed her goodnight, she hugged me tightly and said, "Thanks for getting me through the rough spots." That was really a beautiful moment. She was grateful to be listened to and respected for how she felt. What a dear she is.

I now had a different mother. With her resiliency fading, I no longer took for granted her ability to take care of herself, to bounce back from a low point, or do what she did in the past. She used to look forward to visiting nearby Spring Lake and often brought young grandchildren there. When in conversation, she talked easily and readily. Each night she stayed up late. Now all of that changed. She became quieter, went to bed early, and showed little interest in going to the park.

As much as I desired to bring my mother comfort with things she previously enjoyed, for the most part those disappeared during her remaining three years. I tried again to take her to Spring Lake several months later but by then she could hardly get out of the car and walk to a park bench. Thirty minutes of sitting there was as much as she could handle. I sensed she agreed to go mainly because she thought I wanted her to do so. That was when I acknowledged the part in me, (in all of us, perhaps), that desires a beloved person to maintain their usual persona, to stay the way we've known them. Some part of us cries out, "Please, don't change." We long for their happiness, but can unknowingly resist or miss their compulsory transition in lifestyle and daily habit. It's not just *their* recognition and acceptance of physical and mental limitations that is required. It is vital that *we* adjust to those alterations, too.

Beneath aging's required adjustment of identity lies an adamant voice. This voice continually cries out to the person in elderhood, "Let go!" This cry will not be stilled until it is acknowledged. Even a whispered or unsure "yes" in the older person can initiate a journey of inner growth. Until that "yes," the option of personal transformation remains dormant. Henry Simmons and Jane Wilson put it this way in *Soulful Aging*: "As long as we keep comparing ourselves to a younger, better self . . . we shortchange the possibilities for becoming an older, wiser one. The wisdom of adaptation begins in the willingness to let go of who we used to be and embrace who we now are."[6]

As I accompanied Mom through the big leap in her identity adjustment, I learned the necessity of respecting an older person's struggle and to be aware of how we younger ones respond to that struggle. While we certainly want to do all we can to alleviate pain of body, mind, and spirit in our elders, we often end up needing to say our own "yes." This implies listening without judgment to their emotional and mental reactions, being willing to set aside our hope-filled expectations in order to enter *their* experience, and having enough empathy to recognize what it must be like for them to lose so much of who they thought themselves to be. Above all, companioning our elders requires a wide and deep compassion that allows them to change in ways that may leave us feeling insecure and uncomfortable.

I learned the importance of tending to my own emotional responses to my mother's debilitating health so that I did not foist those emotions upon her. When I learned of Mom's first heart attack I felt numb, in denial and shock. Over and over I wondered if she would recover and, if not, was I prepared to let her go. Mom was so ill during that time and I feared the worst. I dragged my heart around like an old muddy gunny sack, unable to lift the sadness out of it.

The day we met to discuss our mother's home care I noticed she was growing stronger and yet, my dread of her impending death did not lift. That night I wrote in my journal: "I feel in the middle, on a thin rope, wanting to hang onto Mom, yet knowing the hold has to be gentle. I need to be ready to let go, because no matter how strong she gets, she will be weak again."

Ever so slowly, I managed to leave behind my expectations of the mother I used to have. I longed for Mom to move beyond her depression and grief, but I knew it would take time, that nothing I said or did could force its departure. The best gift I could extend was my loving, caring presence. She needed time to adjust and absorb the truth of her diminishment, to find a way to be at peace with herself as she eased into another lifestyle.

I tried to be less anxious about how long it might take for Mom to find that peace, while also doing what I could to ease her angst. I became more patient with the time it took for her to walk from the house to the car or do other easy tasks I took for granted, like readily rising from a chair. I also found ways for her to regain a different sense of purpose. These simple ways proved to be effective. I asked her to pray for me when I traveled on wintry roads or worked on a special project. I valued that support and she felt like she could do something for me, instead of just receiving all the time.

Another way Mom found a sense of satisfaction in doing something of purpose came in opportunities for her to manage certain events. Because she could do so little cooking and liked to entertain, I thought of fixing a luncheon in her home where she could invite whomever she chose. Before I went to buy food she insisted on paying for it. Doing so allowed her to contribute to the luncheon. Everyone enjoyed that get-together and Mom felt contented knowing she played a part in bringing pleasure to others.

One of the requirements of aging involves balancing "doing" with "being." Learning the inherent value of "being" did not come easily for my mother. Because of her sense of unworthiness, she failed to realize how others valued her presence. When I visited, I tried to express how much just being with her meant to me. I constantly assured her that she did not have to *do* anything in order for me to appreciate her. Mom thought her ability to have purpose had deserted her, but her supreme generosity of being a caring, praying, loving presence yielded tremendous benefit for others. This quality of presence can be one of the greatest offerings of the later years. For those who move into elderhood, especially those who have identified themselves by what they have accomplished, it takes time to accept this.

Mom's depression held on for almost a year. Eventually she regained her interest in enjoyable activities like working crossword puzzles, writing letters, and sending cards. By the following spring she no longer needed oxygen, began driving again, and attended various social functions. As she slowly moved out of her slump, countless emotional and physical ups and downs kept yanking her back and forth. She used to have a moderate disposition. Now when I called, her voice might sound light and happy one time, withdrawn and sad the next. Of course, grief is like that, one briefly feels better and then all is gloom.

The same roller coaster happened physically. Just when Mom seemed to be doing well, a new medical problem arose. As Mom recuperated from these episodic illnesses and the heart attack, her doctor advised repeatedly that she "slow down." She didn't listen to that advice very well once she started feeling better. Instead, she tended to overdo it in her desire to live life as fully as possible. Another illness or ailment followed each improvement period. She did well one month and seemed headed toward imminent death the next; she was hospitalized with pneumonia one week and two months later went to a casino. It was not unusual for me to receive a phone call soon after I found her in relatively better health telling me of yet another reversal.

Mom's first heart attack took place in April, three years before her death. In December she was back in intensive care due to fluid on her heart. She returned home a week later, only to fall while going into church the following Sunday—another indication of the continued weakening of her body. Ten days after finally turning a corner after her second heart attack she developed some type of amoebic dysentery that left her with such severe stomach pains the local hospital flew her to a larger one in Sioux City. Up and down, back and forth, so went Mom's passages from a semblance of better health to the possibility she would not leave the hospital alive.

As I listen now to my friends talk about their experience of aging parents and relatives, I hear this same unpredictability of the aging process. It is to be expected— yet one continues to hope *that this time* things will level off, *this time* there will be no more emergencies or reason for concern for a long time. *This* time, the old identity will be restored.

How easy it is to deceive one's self about the tight grip old age has on those we love.

CHAPTER 9

CLIPPED WINGS

Clipped Wings

How did it come to this?

A forced landing, weakened wings
crippled and cropped with age,
a solid source of former strength,
taking you through
dark clouds and heavy downpours.

Those resilient wings assured your
bodily independence
as you soared through storms,
high winds battering
and pressing upon your life.

Now those same weathered wings
bear evidence of missing feathers,
thinning bones and shrunken wingspan,
no longer able to lift and soar
or glide with the gusto that carried
you through turbulent tempests.

Slowly, slowly you learn to accept
those clipped wings, to be content

with nesting in the arms of elderhood.

You submit to this final appendage
of your journey, bid farewell
to cherished autonomy
and slowly fold your worn wings
in peaceful surrender.

—**Joyce Rupp**

On the front cover was a photograph of [Robert]
Graves as a young man: black-haired, handsome, and
full of vitality and hope. My father turned the book
over to show a photograph of the present-day Graves:
hair white, face wrinkled, eyes shrouded in sorrow . . .
"Look at this," my father said . . . "You can't understand
this."

—**Lewis Richmond**
Aging as a Spiritual Practice

What serves as inner strength during one period of life
can become a liability in another. My mother's strong
independence contributed greatly to her self-confidence
during earlier difficulties of her life. With cumulative
physical debility this independence became the very thing
that kept her from inner harmony because she fought
so hard to keep her former verve. This struggle took
emotional energy from her already depleted supply.

My hospice training emphasized how important it is
that persons with increasing diminishment have as much
opportunity and freedom as possible in choosing and
making decisions regarding their life. As Mom's health
declined, I discovered that the ability to control what one
desires gradually shrinks because certain health factors
restrict that possibility.

Being with my mother in her ever-changing medical
situation helped me understand why older people become
discouraged or upset with themselves—or others—when
they reach the stage where they can no longer rely on their

own limbs for support, keep forgetting names or scheduled events, cannot read due to vision impairment, strain to hear what others are saying, lose strength to open a pill bottle or a milk carton, get confused managing finances, and are unable to reach the bathroom or bathe without some assistance. These limitations, among others, typically do not happen all at once. But whatever the timing, they rip the heart out of one's independence.

No matter how much of an effort we make to maintain the fundamental criterion of preserving independence and control, there usually comes a time when an aging person faces dependence on others. To resist or ignore this reality only increases anxiety and distress. I noticed this with Mom during one of her hospitalizations for pneumonia when she grew increasingly restless and anxious to be back home. She detested being in the hospital. Although rarely complaining about the care she received, Mom often voiced a longing to go home—whether the stay was long or short. In her weakened condition with pneumonia, going home was not an option. I thought maybe talking with Mom about her resistance might help alleviate a bit of impatience, so one day I probed a little deeper as to why she loathed being there.

Mom's honesty touched me as she expressed the helpless feeling she experienced in the hospital. She ended her disclosure by saying, "I hate not being able to do things for myself." Ah, there it was, the root cause of the restlessness and resistance. More than discomfort or concern about the illness itself, she dreaded the short-circuiting of her autonomy.

As I observed my mother's struggle to continue taking care of herself without anyone's assistance, I thought of the strong spirit that developed as a young woman tending to her motherless siblings. During this period, Mom's independence thrived. No matter what kind of hardship, illness, or loss came along in her life after that, she managed a way through it. This ability of hers grew stronger after Dad's death when she grew accustomed to managing her own finances, making big decisions like leaving the farm and buying a condominium, deciding how she lived and where she went. All of this was hers to manage. Gradually, the strong winds of aging threatened to undo her independence. Each damaging illness and health crisis robbed her of control over her life, bit by bit.

That tenacity showed up one summer when a big reunion on her side of the family was about to take place. A few days before the Wilberding relatives gathered she had severe heart pain and difficulty breathing. After a visit to the doctor and some tests, he explained, "Hilda, the bottom half of your heart is hardly working. You need to come in tomorrow and have a pacemaker put in." She listened politely and then replied, "Dr. Veit, my sister from California arrives tomorrow. I've not seen her for a long time. I'll have that surgery done after she leaves next week. If God wants me to live until that time, I will." Her doctor expressed concern about her decision and tried to convince

Mom to have the surgery done right away. She listened and then chose to ignore his advice.

Mom lived to receive the pacemaker. This reinforced her belief about being fully in charge of her life. Although this theory worked for a while, she finally had to accept certain changes in order to continue living alone. After the first heart attack, she began wearing a small Life-Alert medical device. If she fell or found herself in any situation that required medical help, she could push the button and trained personnel soon arrived. Wearing this device meant she stayed in her own residence and kept a goodly amount of independence.

As the hospitalizations increased, Mom returned to her home each time less able to take care of it. When any of us children mentioned having someone come in to clean, she insisted this help was unnecessary. It took a while but eventually she agreed. I knew Mom had accepted being assisted in this way when a tall woman slipped into the pew in front of us in church one Sunday. Mom leaned over to me and whispered with a smile, "There's my cleaning lady." Not only did Marge do the housecleaning, she also eased a bit of my mother's loneliness by providing enjoyable conversation while she worked.

Meals on Wheels led to yet another concession regarding her independence. This service, too, Mom initially rejected as unnecessary, but once the meals came on a regular basis, how gladly she welcomed them. Obtaining those daily lunches meant she received good nutrition and could let go of the exhausting tasks of grocery shopping and food preparation.

Getting hearing aids added another notch in Mom's belt of aging. In her mid-thirties, the hearing in her left ear deteriorated due to a firecracker gone awry at a Fourth of July party. As she inched her way into her late seventies the hearing in both ears worsened until she could catch little of what others said. What a difference it made for communication when Mom wore her hearing aids—but there she was again, dependent upon one more thing.

Using a walker also proved to be unacceptable. If special medical situations required using one Mom obediently did so, having no choice during recovery from knee replacements and heart attacks. Using a cane was another matter. She didn't want to be seen leaning on "one of those things" in public and wouldn't use one at home, either. "Those are for old people," she'd say, even though she was in her eighties. A cane or a walker indicated, of course, a certain modicum of dependency. I used to chide Mom, "Oh, just accept using that cane as a part of life. No one is going to think any less of you." But now that I am inching toward the years when a cane or a walker might be my lot in life, I wish my mother were here. I'd apologize for my nagging.

Sometimes the smallest item serves to remind a person of declining physical freedom. The year before Mom died, my sister Sue and I were in the kitchen preparing lunch. We happened to find a dried-up potato under the sink. We hee-hawed about how old it looked and went into the living room to show the wizened thing to Mom, thinking she'd have a good laugh with us. But she barely managed a thin smile. I immediately felt sorry for our careless humor, seeing how our find under the sink humiliated her. Having been a meticulous housekeeper in her active years, our mother could no longer maintain that cleanliness. The fossilized potato symbolized her shriveling ability to get down on her knees to see what lay beneath the sink.

Vulnerability and humility accompany dependency. This became evident when Mom joined me on a trip to speak in Wisconsin. Even with her "new knees," she was having some trouble with walking and balance, but that didn't stop her from traveling along. While I tended to the workshop, she planned to visit a grandson. When Mike came in his rickety truck to take her to his home I noticed his vehicle did not have a running board to get in on the passenger side. I wondered how Mom would ever manage to step that high and get in without one. Mike took care of that problem by pushing her chubby behind into the truck and onto the seat. She laughed about it and never let on that she might be embarrassed. Trying to make light of things—that's how Mom handled a lot of uncomfortable situations.

A much more helpless moment occurred on that same trip. From Wisconsin, Mom and I headed to Illinois where a granddaughter lived. On the way we stopped overnight at a motel. The next day I wanted her to have enough time to shower and dress in privacy so I went for my usual morning walk while she used the bathroom. Midway through the walk I felt a jolting sense of urgency to return to our room. I turned around and raced back. Sure enough, as I opened the door I heard Mom's voice crying out, "Joyce! Joyce!"

I rushed into the bathroom to find her heavy, naked body lodged tightly between the bathtub and the toilet, a result of slipping as she got out of the shower. She looked so distraught and helpless. How pained I felt for her in that predicament. I worried she might be seriously hurt as I tugged and pulled to disengage her from that awkward position. I finally managed to lift her up from the floor. She chipped a shoulder in that slip, but there were no broken bones. Both of us were badly shaken by that incident.

The fall in the motel bathroom initiated future situations where Mom faced discomfiting circumstances. On another trip, this one driving to Montana for a wedding, I thought she'd enjoy traveling through the Bighorn Mountains on the way. I proceeded to drive higher and higher on a narrow road. I planned to keep going but I screeched to a halt when she warned in a tight voice, "Please, stop! If you go any further, I'll have to get out of the car." I looked over to see a sickly pallor on her face. Only later did I discover that heart pain, not fear of safety, led her to cry out in fear. Once again, she had to swallow her pride. She, who revealed such resiliency in the past, now could not tolerate the height of a mountain road. Not only that, she had to rely on me to stop and turn around to ease her pain.

Much of Mom's vulnerability came when she needed to receive physical help. The first time she asked me to cut her toenails she apologized profusely, worrying her feet smelled even though she'd taken extra care to wash them thoroughly. I felt honored to help my mother, grateful to do something she could not do for herself. I knew how much humility it took for her to ask me to do that simple task.

Some of those nails were thick with fungus, orange-colored and ugly looking, making them difficult to clip. I feared I would snip one of her toes in the process of kneeling there, holding her foot in one hand, the clippers in the other, trying my best to be as steady as possible. I was onto the second foot when she yelped, "Ouch! That's too close!" My heart leapt. Instantly I thought the worst: "What if I cut her toe and it gets infected? What if the cut doesn't heal on her diabetic foot? What if she has to have her foot removed?" I looked up with a contrite smile, "Sorry, Mom. I'm really trying to be careful. I didn't mean to get so close." I continued with a more focused approach and she relaxed a bit.

Those toe-nail cutting times increased Mom's trust in me when other vulnerable times of need arose. Nine months after one of her heart attacks she awoke on Christmas morning and called me into her bedroom. She asked with concern, "Do I smell bad?" I did notice a strange odor. Mom was naked except for her panties and pointed at her belly, "Look at this." She had a huge raw, red spot the size of an iron near her groin. It looked like a huge burn. Neither of us knew what it was. I could tell she was scared. So was I. Off to the emergency room we went, to learn hours later that it was an external yeast infection, most probably caused by the diabetes or antibiotics.

After I took Mom back home I went to pick up a prescription and buy the flannel pajamas the doctor suggested to keep the yeast infection aired out. I'll never forget coming into her bedroom after she put on the pajamas that were much too big for her. When I stood next to her, she whimpered, "I'm so miserable. I don't even like me. I never thought it would be this way." And she began crying. My mother, the strong one, so resilient, crying. Her exposed pain devastated my heart. She quickly pulled herself together after I hugged her and said, "I'm so sorry, Mom." She replied, "It's not your fault. You can't do anything about it." Then she brushed aside her tears and walked away from me.

Before I left to go back to my home the next day she apologized to me, saying "I'm sorry that I spoiled Christmas." I hugged her tightly and tried to console her with "Oh, Mom, you didn't spoil Christmas. It was spoiled for you." But I realized nothing I said would undo that horrible experience of utter vulnerability.

I knew that was true because I had been unable to save her from an earlier experience at the time of her first heart attack. An ambulance rushed her to a hospital in Sioux City on a wintry night. It all happened so fast. I followed behind the ambulance, fearing I'd lose sight of it in the heavily falling snow, not knowing the location of the hospital. Once medical personnel situated Mom in the ICU, I went to stay overnight in the visitors' room nearby.

About 4:00 a.m. a nurse awakened me with a touch on the shoulder and asked me to go be with Mom. There she lay, a crumpled body filled with pain, confused about where she was and why. I held her hand and tried to soothe her as best I could. I thought of how terribly defenseless she looked. Nothing of her resilient self seemed left. Finally she calmed and went to sleep.

The next morning a physician arrived. He stood near the door of the ICU room, never going near the bed. He barked questions at her, but she could hardly answer, still groggy and in pain from the heart attack and ambulance trip, plus a night in strange surroundings. Then the doctor used a sharp, parental voice to give her instructions ending with the cold warning, "You'd better get yourself out of that bed and get walking or you're never going to get better."

I couldn't believe what I heard. I turned to him and explained, "She has degenerative disks in her back and severe arthritis. She can hardly walk. What do you expect?" He just sneered at me like I was an overly protective daughter and walked out of the room. I was in shock and, at the same time, bursting with anger. I hurt for my mother in her defenseless position, having to endure his arrogance. That man knew nothing about the woman he chastened. Resiliency and independence resided in her DNA. She, of all people, would try her utmost to improve her physical condition. I had no doubt about that.

Mom's experience with the uncompassionate physician reinforced my belief that older people who become increasingly dependent require advocacy on their behalf.

They need someone concerned about their best interests to speak for them when they are unable to speak for themselves; someone to make sure their medical condition is understood and that they are not belittled in their defenseless condition.

Another of Mom's humbling times occurred when she could no longer bathe or put on clothes without some help. In May of 1999 when she was in the hospital with one of her bouts of pneumonia, I helped with her sponge bath and accompanied her to the bathroom. That was the day she asked if what I was doing for her resembled what I did as a volunteer for hospice. As I spoke with her about my experience, she seemed to be more at ease with her lack of strength.

Her dependency reminded me of Morrie Schwartz, a sociology professor, who spoke to Mitch Albom in *Tuesdays with Morrie* about his last stages of cancer:

> "I'm an independent person, so my inclination was to fight all of this—being helped from the car, having someone else dress me. I felt a little ashamed, because our culture tells us we should be ashamed if we can't wipe our own behind. But then I figured, forget about what the culture says. I have ignored the culture much of my life. I am not going to be ashamed. What's the big deal? And you know what? The strangest thing."
>
> "What's that?"
>
> "I began to enjoy my dependency. Now I enjoy when they turn me over on my side and rub

cream on my behind so I don't get sores. Or when they wipe my brow, or they massage my legs. I revel in it. I close my eyes and soak it up. And it seems very familiar to me. It's like going back to being a child again. Someone to bathe you. Someone to lift you. Someone to wipe you. We all know how to be a child. It's inside all of us. For me, it's just remembering how to enjoy it."[1]

When Mom needed the kind of help that Morrie describes, my sister Lois provided much of it. She and her husband Jim welcomed our mother into their home during one of Mom's recuperation periods. Lois helped her bathe, gave her back rubs, laid out her clothes, and helped her to dress. Mom received all of this graciously, constantly saying "thank you." She often phrased it this way, "Thanks for waiting on me"—another indication of her keen awareness of being in a receiving posture. She was grateful for every kindness shown and gradually grew in her ability to accept what others did for her. I think it eventually brought our mother pleasure to have someone tend to her after all the years she took care of others.

After being at Lois and Jim's, Mom returned to her condo. I stayed with her for several days while she adjusted to being home. During that time I noticed her pluck, how she tried to do whatever she could for herself. At the same time, I also observed how she became more used to the notion that it was okay to receive from others. On one of those evenings in June, I wrote in my journal: "I see how fragile Mom is and wonder how she'll do it alone in her condo after having lived at Lois and Jim's. She's brave and still wants to be independent but it's hard. I was able to give her a back rub last night when she was in bed; what a privilege to do this for her. Her skin is soft and barely wrinkled. Her face, too, is smooth and hardly blemished. Amazing for all the work she did both indoors and out in the garden. Tomorrow I will help her with her shower."

It was during this time that I also experienced a tender moment of tucking Mom into bed for the night. How fragile and dear she appeared as she lay there without her wig, her soft, thinning, grey-black hair on the pillow. She kissed and hugged me as she bade me good night and sent me forth with, "I love you," after I laid my hand on her head and blessed her, "May the angels watch over you."

Another growth in the area of lessening independence came about as Mom began asking for what she needed emotionally. This first happened when she called and asked if I would be with her during cataract surgery. I sensed she felt some dread about having that simple surgery done. Mom rarely requested anything and tried to handle difficulties by herself, especially if it might cause others inconvenience, so her request seemed especially imperative. She stepped over a big hurdle in asking me to be with her. After that there were times when Mom called just to talk about what troubled her. This might be to have me listen to a hurt or a concern she felt about a personal relationship, or just to talk because it was a lonesome day.

As Mom turned the corner on her former way of being independent and productive, she wisely hung onto some gestures that sustained her ability to give. She had always been generous with however little or much she had. When she could no longer drive to visit a sick friend, go regularly to the nursing home to help with a card party, or bake something for a funeral dinner, she still found a way to be generous. Hardly anyone left her home after a visit without carrying away a gift. This might be cookies someone else baked for her, a new hand towel, one of her prized wedding gifts, a box of stationery, some kitchen item she knew she'd never use again, or a treasured piece of jewelry. "Here," she'd say as she extended the gift, "You might be able to use it," or, "I want you to have this."

Feeling useful brings a sense of satisfaction to all of us and most certainly for older persons whose sense of purpose dwindles with increasing physical restraint. Mom still continually searched for ways to be of use. After recovering from her depression she surprised me by suggesting she donate her body to science. "I can't do much for anyone anymore and I've given a lot of thought to this," she explained. "I hope you'll help me find out what to do." Her consideration of doing this allowed another way for her to feel she could still be in control of some part of her life and also contribute to the benefit of others.

My mother always wanted to help. She would put up with a lot of physical discomfort and personal inconvenience to make someone else feel good. When I arrived at her home the year before her death, Mom stood at the kitchen stove, trying to make one of her homemade soups for my visit. She could hardly stand upright for more than a few minutes without severe back pain, yet she endured that discomfort so she could make something tasty for me to enjoy.

A few months after that visit, Mom traveled with my sister-in-law Opal to go to one of my book signings in Omaha, Nebraska, a hundred and twenty miles away. During that afternoon she sat by my side, happy to be there even though her pale face indicated a body fraught with hurt. At the close of the event, when I leaned over Mom's wheelchair to hug and thank her for coming, she gave me a loving smile and said simply, "I wanted to do it for you."

That one line said so much to me. My mother's wings may have been clipped but her love still soared freely.

CHAPTER 10

The GIFT of THE SUN PORCH

Soul Contractions

My mother ages
all too quickly now,
the latest illness
claiming more chunks
of her vitality each day.

This beloved woman
whose womb held my body,
I now hold
in the chalice of my vigilance.

Sadness and sorrow
pulse inside my spirit,
a kindred soul-contraction
resonating with her spiritual gestation
as she prepares
during these final years
for her birth into eternity.

Dear mother,
I, who burst forth from
your womb
on a sunny morning in June,

embrace you now with gratitude,
praying to let you go freely,

to encourage your spirit
to wing forward peacefully
into the mystery
of the One Great Womb,

where there is space
enough
to embrace us all.

—Joyce Rupp

All the treasures I've gathered
during my lifelong preparation
I'm now arranging for the last day
to give it all to death—
the day death comes to my door.

—Rabindranath Tagore
Show Yourself to My Soul

One of the most supportive kindnesses we can offer to those nearing the end of life is to listen attentively to what they have to say about death. A receptive presence lessens apprehension, strengthens courage, and allows freedom to speak thoughts and feelings about the final departure. This conversation may be uncomfortable, for the loved one who is speaking or the one who will be left behind. No matter how uneasy the emotional response when the topic arises, addressing the reality of dying gives a loved one the reassurance of being heard.

As depression side-swiped my mother's resilient spirit and physical diminishment stole pieces of her independence, she moved steadily toward a recognition of her own impermanence and mortality. She faced what we all eventually meet when moving into the last years of our life and she needed to talk about it.

When in her eighties, Florida Scott-Maxwell penned this reflection in her journal:

> I don't like to write this down, yet it is much in
> the minds of the old. We wonder how much older
> we have to become, and what degree of decay

we may have to endure. We keep whispering
to ourselves, "Is this age yet? How far must I
go?" For age can be dreaded more than death.
"How many years of vacuity? To what degree of
deterioration must I advance?" Some want death
now, as release from old age, some say they will
accept death willingly, but in a few years. I feel
the solemnity of death, and the possibility of
some form of continuity. Death feels a friend
because it will release us from the deterioration
of which we cannot see the end. It is waiting for
death that wears us down, and the distaste for
what we may become.[1]

Questions similar to those of Maxwell's swirled around
in my mother when she turned eighty. I marveled at the
openness with which she carried on conversations about
her ensuing journey into the vast unknown. I tried to listen
carefully when she spoke of her impending death, even
though a huge stone of resistance plunked in my gut as I
thought about what this meant for the future. But I knew
the vital necessity of listening without objection or denial
to what she wanted to say.

I could not do much to assuage Mom's painful crucible
of aging, but my attentive ear and heart could give her
the gift of a caring presence. I had to set aside my own
ego with its longing to have my mother's life continue and
focus, instead, on the reality of which she desired to speak.
Among her various wishes, she asked that a "no code"—do

not resuscitate—be added to her medical records, and she wanted this choice respected.

She went much further than this decision, however. Unbeknownst to any of us children, at age eighty-two she drove to the local mortuary where she took care of details for her funeral. I heard about this when I sat across from Mom at the breakfast table. She announced, in a matter of fact tone, "Last week, I went to Greenwood's and ordered my casket. I paid my bills and took care of other arrangements that needed tending. Now, you kids won't have to worry about doing that." This gesture indicated yet another of her generous gifts to us. Another thoughtful kindness. But this one I found especially painful to accept.

I thought I was comfortable speaking about this topic. I was—as long as it did not include such explicit realism regarding my own mother's demise. In spite of past openness to conversations with her, those words about funeral plans stirred me to attention. Suddenly death seemed much too close. The thought pierced me: "Death will arrive and take her from me." I wanted to protest, "No, Mom, no, don't talk about dying. Not yet. I'm sure you can live a long time." As if, by not talking about the details, it would prevent death's arrival.

In spite of my inner resistance, I entered into the conversation because I knew she needed my open and caring presence. I managed to bypass my emotional reaction and responded instead, "It's hard for me to hear this, but I'm glad you're telling me about it. You have such courage. Thank you for going ahead with all of that, Mom.

You're a great example to the rest of us about how to face the future."

Mom's decision to go to the Greenwood Funeral Home did not come instantly. Considerable inner turmoil and eventual reconciliation led up to that visit. She found the strength and freedom to do so only after the excruciating depression had lifted and she had won her struggle to let go of the energetic independence that shaped her life. Once she made the decision to face the truth of her mortality, she leaned into it without self-pity or hesitation. Mom approached this as she had done throughout life's challenges, with a resolute attitude and a courageous heart. Fortitude and determination allowed her to do what many elderly shun.

Some senior people never want to talk about death. They do not want the subject brought up and reject any sign of its imminence. They certainly do not choose to make plans regarding their funeral. Other aged people's response goes to the opposite extreme. They talk about death all the time. (These people often end up "dying" long before their last breath.) Still others, like my mother, face this reality head on, allow sufficient preparation for its arrival, and then continue to cherish and enjoy what remains in life. Mom did not intend to stop living while death approached. Whenever she could she took part in social gatherings. And of course, she made as many monthly trips to "the boat" as her body allowed. Some of her zest for life had been vacuumed out of her spirit, but once she made peace with what lay ahead she gathered all the gusto she could and enjoyed each day to the fullest.

I never heard my mother express anxiety or dread regarding her mortality. When she finally acquiesced to her clipped wings, she accepted the inevitability of her worn-out body, knowing it could not serve her sufficiently much longer. Personal faith and beliefs helped greatly as she leaned into this peaceful acceptance. She looked forward to seeing her husband again and her many relatives and friends who had departed before her. Mom's history of resilience contributed greatly to her peace, but one very specific period in her early eighties led to the necessary surrender that the end of life requires.

This amazing event took place on my sister and brother-in-law's sun porch while Mom lived with them for five weeks recuperating from one of her heart attacks. After Lois and Jim left for work, Mom basically had the day to herself. Lois came home at noon to share lunch and check to see if all was well, but the day included lots of solitude. I still remember the calm, satisfied way Mom described this contemplative experience. A small, three-season porch on Lois and Jim's home faced the south. Several tall oak trees stood across the street. On the porch Mom found a welcoming bench where she sat contentedly for hours with the warm, comforting sun bathing her. When Mom described that scene later on, she said, "I just sat there and thought about my life and what may become of me. I loved the sun and the quiet. It felt so good."

The solitude and stillness allowed Mom to go deeper inside, to let go of her former identity and step into her new skin. In *Emptiness Dancing*, Adyashanti writes, "I think there is nothing we, as human beings, resist more than a spiritual winter. If humans did not resist the stripping away of their own identities and allowed themselves to experience winter time, we would all be enlightened. If we just let wintertime dawn in us, there is a natural stripping away, more like a falling away. When you are still and quiet, falling away happens naturally."[2]

During her quiet reflection on the sun porch my mother took a long look at her "wintertime." Like the character Jamie in Zora Neale Hurston's novel *Their Eyes Were Watching God* who "saw her life like a great tree in leaf with the things suffered, things enjoyed, things done and undone,"[3] so, too, with Mom. Much "falling away" happened as she reflected on her tree of life during this graced interval. She remembered and pondered who and what she valued, and how much her faith meant to her. In doing so, she made a decision to give herself to the emptying that death demands. Her spirit was ripe for responding to this stripping away.

Until those transforming days at Lois and Jim's, Mom lived an extroverted life. Not that she denied having an inner self, she simply chose to focus on the exterior one. When she entered into the contemplative silence of the sun porch, she discovered what Michael Himes concludes in his essay "The Suffering of Christ":

Old people, and all of us get older every day, ought to be explorers. There is new and unexplored territory before us—unexplored, at least, by me. I know what it is like to grow, now I must learn what it is like to fade. I know what it is like to be born, now I must find out what it is like to die. Such exploration requires remaining still . . . because it is a matter not of going out but of going in—moving into that vast desolation, the vast, cold waters of the petrel and porpoise. We learned that long ago on the banks of the Jordan and in the Garden of Gethsemane.[4]

Mom's "Gethsemane" came about in her depression and the radical slowing down of her active life. She did not want what was happening to her anymore than Jesus wanted his suffering. She recognized her waning lifespan and gradually slipped into peace about it when she entered the interiority which Himes describes. She found in those deep waters the acceptance she needed to say with firm faith, "Yes, your will be done both in my life and in my death."

When Mom sifted and sorted through the long journey of her life, she entered a contemplative space that allowed her to let go more fully of her valued productivity, to release her past identity as an active, in-charge woman. With nothing to "do," except sit in the sun porch, she could turn toward the deepest part of her being. In this solitude, she found acceptance of a new identity, that of "being" rather than "doing." There she received reassurance that all would be well when she took her last breath. What a graced moment. With her hand clasped in the Giver of Life's, she pondered her personal journey and trusted all would be well when her physical self ceased to be.

Once Mom gave herself to her final journey this did not lessen her enthusiasm for life. She still found reasons for joy and gratitude in each day. I learned this during her sojourn at Lois and Jim's when I visited her. As I kissed Mom good night, she said, "As I tell Lois, another good day of life." Mom's gratitude seemed to enlarge daily and she easily shared her appreciation with others. Later that year when we had another open talk about death she assured me, "I'm not afraid to die but I enjoy living each day." I learned from Mom's surrender to death not to cling or grasp at life but, equally, to relish and taste it as fully as possible.

When Mom returned to her condominium, she brought home a different spirit. Her voice held a softer, easier sound when she mentioned physical limitations. She stopped referring to herself as "lazy" and no longer voiced irritation about unrelenting infirmities. This change included more than resignation. Her indication of how much she liked a poem by Jessica Powers convinced me of the internal transformation taking place.

Mom had never expressed an interest in poetry. I would not have considered giving her the poem, but she happened to find a copy of it in a book I loaned her. "Remarkable," I thought, as she expressed an appreciation of Powers' words. After I re-read the poem, I understood why it resonated with Mom.

The gesture of a gift is adequate.
If you have nothing: laurel leaf or bay,
no flower, no seed, no apple gathered late,
do not in desperation lay
the beauty of your tears upon the clay.

No gift is proper to a Deity.
No fruit is worthy for such power to bless.
If you have nothing, gather back your sigh,
and with your hands held high, your heart held high,
lift up your emptiness![5]

My mother found a kindred spirit in Jessica Powers. She knew that kind of emptiness, knew how "having nothing" felt. Few of her friends were still alive. Her body did not work very well. Her energy sagged a little more each day and her memory began to let her down. She recognized less and less of the woman she used to be. Like the poet, Mom could bring her nothingness to God and still have a high heart. From this realization came a willingness to surrender to the inevitable, to believe she would be okay. This surrender led to the peace Mom brought back with her after living with Lois and Jim.

Out of this transformation came a desire to live as unencumbered as possible. Had Mom known May Sarton's poetry, she would have found another kindred spirit. In *At Seventy*, Sarton wrote about this same desire: "The clutter falls away. The non-essential things cease to trouble the mind."[6] Mom felt similarly and found that material items she once enjoyed were not that important anymore. When

Christmas and birthday celebrations approached, she entreated, "Please stop giving me things." This detachment is difficult for younger people to acknowledge. In hoping to show love, we children struggled with how to honor our mother's request. We still continued to give what she really did not need or want until, finally, we came up with *the perfect gift*.

Ever since our days on the farm, we knew how much our mother loved flowers. We could count on rows of cosmos, zinnia, gladiolus, snap-dragon, sweet-pea, and tall hollyhocks bordering her vegetable garden. Brilliant blue irises lined the west side of the house in the spring and golden pansies on the north. A patch of moss roses and bright scarlet salvia met visitors who came to the front door in the summer. Some flowers Mom picked and brought indoors, particularly her beloved roses that grew by the south side of the house, but most of the flowers were to be enjoyed where they grew. Thus, it came to be that we children decided to gift our aging mother with a bouquet of fresh flowers each month. Oh, how happy Mom felt about this gift. She would wait expectantly for the flowers to arrive and then phone us to describe with elation the kind and color. When the flowers began to fade, she created smaller and smaller bouquets with the ones that remained fresh. It took so little to bring our mother happiness.

As Mom continued in an effort to simplify her life, she marked people's names on the bottom of items they gave her through the years so these things could be returned to the giver after she died. She also stopped purchasing clothes. When it came to making plans for an event or any type of travel further than a week ahead, she wouldn't set a date. She dismissed it with, "We'll see when the time gets closer." I thought Mom to be overly-cautious. I see now she was being realistic.

This practical approach, based on the tangible possibility of not being around much longer, began while living with Lois and Jim. She decided to not connect the Life-Alert medical device which she wore at home. I presumed this was because of the cost, but no, it was mostly about recognizing the impermanence of her life. When I asked Mom about the decision, she said matter-of-factly, "When you get to be eighty-three, it really doesn't make that much difference."

Thoughts of her mortality had became more pronounced when Mom turned eighty. That year, she surprised us by having a professional photo taken to give us at Christmas. She looked pretty with her carefully placed makeup and a lovely blue dress. Was she thinking about dying and wanting to have an up-to-date photo? This didn't occur to me at the time, but now I wonder if this might have been the reason behind that gift.

Mom's recognition of approaching of death also showed itself in how much she talked about Dad and other deceased loved ones. In her last year she often mentioned dreaming about Lester. From the way she spoke about these night visits, she anticipated a joyful reunion. One morning she described him in a dream of the previous evening: "He had a white shirt, no tie. Coat jacket and slacks. He was in the corner of the room. We were at a party. He came over to me and said, 'Isn't it time we go home?' We left. I brought him to the condo. He said how much he liked it." Dreams of this nature sometimes visit those approaching death, reminding them of their imminent departure. This dream seemed to assure Mom she was ready to "go home."

Another indication of her insightful awareness of her last days revealed itself in Mom's telling Lois she did not lock the front door of her condo at night—"just in case someone would need to come in and find me." During that same time, Mom told me how much she liked *May I Walk You Home?*, which Joyce Hutchison and I wrote to aid those accompanying someone nearing their final days.[7] Mom liked it so much that she took copies of the book to her cardiac therapy nurses. In so many ways my mother tried to communicate a message to us: "I don't think I am going to be here much longer."

As Mom grew in accepting what lay ahead, I thought I was gradually accepting her future death, too. Anticipatory grief, that's what the experts call it—saying a final farewell in bits and pieces before the end actually arrives. I believed I was doing that. Perhaps I was. Yet, I was far from being finished with the process. My head prepared to say goodbye but my heart lagged far behind.

Each time I visited Mom I bid her farewell with a growing confidence that I could let go of her when it was time, even though I always wondered as I drove away, "Will this be the last time?" At that stage, she couldn't even make it to the door when I left because it was too difficult to get out of her chair. So sure was I of my ability to face impending relinquishment that the last time I saw Mom alive, I left feeling less sad about having to go, assuring myself I would be alright if I could not see her again. I loved my mother but wanted to be ready for her death because I knew *she* was ready. I forgot that it's one thing to intellectualize readiness and quite another to feel it. How wrong I was to think I would not need to grieve my mother's absence when she died.

In February, two months before Mom passed on, I spent a weekend with her. In helping to make her bed, I noticed the mattress needed replacing. She didn't want a new one and said something to the effect that she wasn't going to be around that long. I denied that possibility with, "Oh, no, you're going to be here for a long time." Immediately, her face sort of crumpled. I can see that change even now. It was as if she suddenly set aside a waterfall of tears. She caught herself and recovered enough to say, "Well, maybe two years." She knew by her body's responses and her spirit's intuition she did not have long to live. I totally missed what she wanted so much for me to acknowledge. How disappointed she must have been to have me deny her coming death when we had such good conversations about it in the past.

Deny it, I did. Six months before Mom's departure a little melody leapt into my mind repeatedly on my walks, in meditation, when driving, or anytime I wasn't focusing intently on work. I didn't know the source of the song or any of the words other than "Soon, soon, and very soon." I had little inkling of why the words pursued me.

A few months after Mom's death, quite "by accident," I came across the song by Andraé Crouch, *Soon and Very Soon*, and gasped at the lyrics: "Soon and very soon we're going to see the King. No more crying there, No more dying there, we're going to see the King." The song was about death! In those months before she died, the silent voice of the Holy One tried to prepare me to let go—but I unconsciously shoved that strong nudge aside in my reluctance to say farewell.

Mom lived until April 20. This happened to be Holy Thursday, four days before Easter, the hope-filled feast of Jesus being raised from the dead. In mid-morning of that day a call came from my sister-in-law Opal telling me, "The doctor said to notify the children. Mom's not going to make it." Opal explained that the night before Mom had developed severe pain in her left leg which turned out to be a blood clot. True to our mother's history of endurance, she toughed it out that night. The next morning she needed hospitalization and soon after being admitted, her doctor recognized the end was near.

"Happy Easter." These were Mom's last words—the final gift she offered, spoken to Father Gene Sitzmann, a former pastor who came to anoint Mom with the blessed oils for the sick and dying. Although her greeting came out in a weak whisper, it was accompanied with a tender smile. With only a few hours before leaving us behind, she still managed to be gracious and thoughtful to someone else.

And she must have recognized her own Easter was near at hand.

Death did not wait long. An hour or so later, Mom departed. Those who were present noticed how peaceful she seemed during those remaining hours of life. Here was the great leave-taking for which Hilda Rupp had readied. With strong faith, she embraced this ending, not fearing what was to be. In *The Heart of God*, Rabindranath Tagore prays, "Let this be my last word, that I trust in Your love."[8] Mom trusted. She went easily into the Holy One's loving embrace. Shortly after Father Sitzmann left, she turned onto her right side and detached from those in the room. Her eyes became riveted, looking beyond into the distance, complete attention given to what those in the room could not behold. Did she see her beloved mother, lost to her for sixty-seven years? Were her husband and son David beckoning? Surely her many deceased friends gathered among those urging her homeward, "Come, come, Hilda, we've been waiting for you."

I'll always be grateful to my sister Lois for asking the hospital staff to wait for my arrival before removing Mom's body. When I walked into the room a half hour after her death, my brother-in-law Jim said, "She's gone." My heart plummeted. Gone? Where? Where are you, Mom? I don't want you *gone*. Not yet. Not now. I went to the bed where my mother's inert body lay, her limbs still warm. She was slightly curled in a cocoon-like position. I stroked her thin, damp hair, held her face in my hands and kissed her goodbye. But this time my mother did not respond.

Silence. Dead. Gone. I tried my utmost to accept that my resilient mother was no longer there. Only later that day did I consider how the empty shell of her body suggested the translucent sheath that a butterfly leaves behind when it takes flight. Then I recalled a conversation of ours four months earlier. Mom had leaned over the Scrabble board that night and announced, "You know I'm not afraid of dying." I thought, "Where did that come from all of a sudden?" I said out loud, "Well, Mom, I'm really glad to hear that, but I want you around for a long time." She smiled her endearing smile and said with characteristic good humor, "Well, just make sure I have my wings on when I go!"

As if in confirmation that she had gained those fresh wings of freedom, two butterflies flitted by when we turned to leave the cemetery after her funeral several days later. I smiled at the thought of my mother leaving this world with new wings, strong and free, carrying her to a long-awaited destination.

CHAPTER 11

A BOOK *of* REGRETS

The Hungry Lion

Regret
stalks like a hungry lion,
invading memories,
devouring joy
while recrimination
drools with satisfaction.

It is time
to tame the hungry lion
with self-forgiveness,
accept the truth
of having done one's best,
move beyond remorse
and the futility
of trying to change the past.

Turn inward toward
a love bigger than regret,
stride up to the hungry lion,
sniff the rancid breath
of 'could have, would have,
should have, ought to have,'

and all the wishes of how to undo
what was, or was not done.

Take a deep inhalation,
look the hungry lion
in the eye,
let out a long, cleansing sigh
and welcome the freedom
that comes with letting go.

—**Joyce Rupp**

We all encounter situations in our lives
where we wish we hadn't done something we did,
or wish we had done something we didn't.
                    —Marianne Williamson
                        A Return to Love

Reviewing the past is a natural activity as one ages. When Mom looked back on her life, she found things she regretted. She talked to me about some of those qualms of conscience, especially her approach to disciplining us eight children. My brother David, the fourth oldest and the one who drowned at age twenty-three, exhibited an over-abundance of energy in his youth. He would probably now be diagnosed as having attention deficit disorder. With three other small children to care for and a list of endless daily tasks, Mom tied a rope around Dave's waist and attached the rope to one of the trees in the front yard. This leash-like rope allowed enough room for him to play but not to get away. Looking back, Mom felt badly about doing this. I assured her that she, like many parents, did the best she could under the circumstances. She did not do it to be mean or cruel to Dave. She simply acted to keep him from running away or being hurt.

Mom also expressed remorse over the way she disciplined by spanking or using a hair brush to whack us on the bottom. She looked, too, at what she failed to do because of how busy she kept at home. "Oh, how I wish I could have spent more time reading and playing with you kids," she remarked one day.

Whenever we discussed her regrets it seemed to relieve Mom's concern and lessen the intensity and power these negative parts of the past held over her. I found this to be true in Mom's situation and I've found it to be true in my own. I've learned since her death that unhealed self-accusation can tear apart a mind, drown good memories, and conjure up guilt powerful enough to paralyze the natural process of grief.

There are those who glide smoothly beyond the past. They rarely look back and move into the future without much concern about what they might have done differently. When I inquired with an acquaintance about anything she wished she could have changed regarding her father's death, she remarked, "What's done is done. I can't undo it. So why hang on?" That response intensified my sense of failure. Not only did I have regrets, her comment left me feeling I should be able to leave them behind without a second thought. Unfortunately, in regard to my mother, my heart got snagged. It took quite a while, ten years to be exact, to untangle the guilt and remorse I felt after she died.

I found some compassion for that emotional snag when I asked a friend if she had any regrets after a beloved person in her life succumbed to cancer. My friend faced me with honest eyes and admitted, "I was a book of regrets." I knew my friend had eventually moved on from her grief, so that reply comforted me. Knowing someone else went through painful misgivings didn't take away my remorsefulness but it did, somehow, give me valuable courage to face what I lamented. And it gave me hope. I somehow knew I could ultimately leave my self-imposed recriminations behind.

My "book of regrets" contained more sorrow than guilt over what I felt I had failed to do, as well as what I *did* do and wished I had not. The litany of these incidents stretched out in a long line. Some were ridiculously tiny situations, like chiding Mom for throwing her chewing gum in a pool of water in a national park. Others were bigger: "If only I had listened more closely, not denied her impending death, called more often, stayed longer when I visited, been with her before she took her last breath."

Whatever the size, each supposed failure loomed like an ominous thundercloud—threatening at times to engulf my thoughts and emotions with a flood of fresh sadness. Always I wished I would have *been more, done more.* And yet, I was a good daughter and 95 percent of the time a dear friend to my mother. While my self-reproaches no longer consume me, I tell of them here in hope that the telling lessens the distress of others who bear the burden of their own regrets, especially in regard to aging and end-of-life issues.

After Mom's death, my remembrance of the tough things she went through in her physical diminishment kept surfacing. As these memories arose, I blamed myself for a lack of empathy and for my insensitivity about aging. The memory of being with her for dinner with some of my other siblings where we all chided her about going to cardiac rehab and being emphatic about her need to exercise saddened me. Later that same evening, she was so tired when we returned to her home she could barely talk. She went straight to bed. I didn't comprehend the scope of her exhaustion until the next morning when she apologized to me for not being more hospitable. She even said she felt guilty and almost got up to talk to me. As I revisited this experience, I felt miserable knowing how I failed in being understanding and compassionate with her that evening.

Sorrow continually surfaced when I recalled my unawareness of what it was like for my mother to have less and less energy. I wished I had been more attentive to how she continually yielded greater portions of her independence as she relied on others for her care. Even though I tried to be there for Mom and wanted to relieve her distress, I felt I could have done much more to help her last years be less difficult.

I regretted not paying closer attention to simple ways of assisting her, such as helping to make her queen-sized bed. She could hardly bear to stand for more than a minute or two without sharp back pain and trouble breathing, so that task took immense energy from her. Only in the last year did I realize she needed my able-bodied help with that strenuous chore.

And, oh, how I longed to have spent more time with my mother; more than just my monthly weekend visits. As I waited in an airport to board a plane a year or so after Mom died, a gate attendant came by pushing a thin, white-haired woman in a wheelchair. Accompanying her was a tall, blond, forty-ish woman who leaned over the elderly woman to kiss her pale cheek. "I'm going to miss you, Mom," she said with a wan smile. Her mother looked up with anticipated loneliness in her voice. "You could come with me," she suggested. Her daughter smiled and chose not to say anything.

At that moment, I felt a sharp pang of memory. I saw those many times my mother stood at the door of her home after we hugged and said our goodbyes. How she would stand there, wave, and force a smile as I backed my car out of the driveway. Never one to cling, Mom did not beg or whine. She would simply say with love in her voice, "We had such a good time. I hope you will come back soon."

The thought of not having spent more time with Mom created my greatest distress. I had to forgive myself for selfishly hurrying back to what I thought was of utmost importance—my work and its success—or for sometimes choosing not to visit at all. Like Mother's Day the year before her death. It was the first weekend that I didn't have to travel in over a month. I decided to take the day for some recovery time instead of driving the five-hour round trip to Omaha where my siblings gathered to celebrate with Mom. What a different choice I would have made had I known it would be the last Mother's Day of her life.

Eventually, I also gave myself some slack with the acknowledgment that there is nothing wrong with taking care of oneself. I knew, too, that I went regularly to visit Mom. I loved her dearly, enjoyed our time together and wanted to be with her. Visiting her posed no problem. What finally freed me from this burdened sorrow was when I accepted that I tried to do the best I could. I knew this to be true.

Another of my big self-reproaches concerned how I responded when Mom confided her fear of going to a nursing home. She detested the thought that this might happen. She ended the conversation by saying, "Aunt Rita's children told her they'll never put *her* in a nursing home."

I took a deep breath and thought anxiously, "Now, what do I say?" One thing was certain. I was determined to be honest.

"Oh, Mom," I replied, "Aunt Rita's children can't promise that. There may come a time when they have no choice. None of us children want you to be in a nursing home. I know we'll do everything we can to keep you from it. But the time may come when we'll have no other choice." Her face fell with disappointment, like a prison door clanging shut.

I thought my honesty to be the right approach, but after Mom died four months later, I wished I had not spoken as I did. First of all, I assumed I knew why she didn't want to go to the nursing home. How helpful it would have been for her to be able to talk about her reluctance and concerns. Instead, I leapt right in with a response. I was sorry that I didn't tell her we'd do the same as Aunt Rita's children. This response would have alleviated Mom's concerns and given her peace. Instead she continued to carry that yoked fear.

Eben Alexander, author of *Proof of Heaven*, writes, "I've always believed that when you're under the burden of a potentially fatal illness, softening the truth is fine. To prevent a terminal patient from trying to grab on to a little fantasy to help them deal with the possibility of death is like withholding pain-killing medication."[1] The same might be true in responding to an elder person's dread of going to a nursing home.

What relief it would have been for my mother to hear that she could stay in her own home. Would that I had been less concerned about "being honest" and more concerned about her peace of mind and heart. If the time came when the only choice meant her moving to a nursing home, that would have been the time to deal with the tough reality. As it turned out, we never had to do that.

One other regret that loomed large focused on my not arriving in time to be there when Mom died. I blamed myself for getting there a half-hour late. A continually rising thought plagued me: "I could have gotten there before she died if I had just hurried more quickly." My sister-in-law's call sounded urgent, but I had known similar phone messages about Mom when she suffered her heart attacks. Each time Mom survived. Even if she was really dying this time, I counted on the process taking a few days, maybe even weeks. I lived a hundred and eighty miles away, so I took time to pack a suitcase and prepare to be away for a while.

Several years earlier when we sat at the breakfast table having one of our many wonderful conversations, death was the subject. Mom assured me she was "ready to go." Because I travel so much for my work, I responded, "You do not need to wait for me if you are ready to take off. I'd love to be there, but it's okay if you need to go without me being there." Little did I know she would take me at my word. I didn't feel bad about giving her that permission, but I deeply regretted my denial that she was really dying. My closed mind and disbelieving heart held me back from accepting how close she was to her last breath. I didn't want to lose my mother, but I had wished so much to be there when she died.

While at Mallard Island ten years later, I found freedom from that nagging regret. I wrote the following one morning: "Yesterday, a healing moment, as I read through the pages of my journal after Mom's death. I chided myself all these years for not hurrying more to get there before she departed. But in my journal I see that I left twenty-five minutes after Opal called. I packed, turned off the computer, and went. I did not tarry long. Even if I had left immediately, I still would not have made it in time."

In those years when remorse threatened to consume me, I tried to stay attentive to its presence even though I sometimes felt it would crush me with its sledge-hammer sadness. I learned a lot from letting my regrets be my unwanted companions. Some of them carried a certain amount of truth and needed to be admitted and forgiven. Others carried falsehood; lies that had to be named and sent away.

As I tended to my regrets, I came to understand the need to free myself from the pain they caused me so that I could cradle the beautiful joy in my memories of Mom.

Francis Weller writes in *Entering the Healing Ground*: "To live with regret is to carry a heavy sadness. It is like walking through a graveyard of loss. However, when regrets are polished by forgiveness and compassion, they can soften and release the life trapped inside."[2]

How true Weller's insight is. There comes a time in grieving when we have to stop dragging our bag of regrets around and lay them aside. I knew the time had come for me to do this. If I allowed my recriminations to poke continually around in my mind and heart, they would consume my self-worth and destroy my memories of the beautiful relationship I enjoyed with Mom. My acquaintance was right. The past cannot be undone. I could acknowledge my deliberate and unintentional failures while also seeing how much I did with and for my mother that was worthy of love.

While the past cannot be undone, I can grow from it. My regrets have motivated me to change my ways. I now make an effort to put people and relationships before work and productivity. I am more attentive to what an older person experiences. I listen closely when they voice fear and concern, and decide carefully before choosing honesty over kindness.

I also remember to gather from the past the good that takes place among the not-so-good. I have discovered that the good things almost always outweigh the scarcity of them. And, perhaps, most significant of all, I've learned how to forgive myself.

TURNING *Toward*
the MORNING

On the Eve of My Mother's Birthday

On the eve of my mother's birthday,
six years after her death,
I rise in the deep of night.

On my way to the bathroom
a wide ray of moonlight
coming through the south window
stuns me with its brilliance.

I move toward its allurement
and stand with full attention
in the gaze
of the strong, full moon,

wondering why I feel blessed,
why this light coming from afar
has the touch of holiness,
why I want to gather it
around me like a sacred womb.

A quiet smile rests on my sleepy face
for I sense a mothering presence

vaster than my small awareness
can even begin to comprehend,

a mystery I step into
for a brief time
before slipping back into bed,

breathing dreams
I leave behind
when I awake to the forgetfulness
of another day.

—Joyce Rupp

And he stood slowly for he was old now, and
ambled away.

—Mary Oliver
"Good-bye Fox"

One morning Mary Oliver notices an old fox lying in the
shade of a tree. The fox sees her but does not hurry away.
The poet and the fox openly observe one another. After a
bit of this mutual attentiveness, the fox slowly gets up and
leaves.

I found Oliver's poem about the fox while I was
writing the first chapter of this memoir. The description
could easily apply to my mother in her final years. Like
the old fox, so my aging mother met her transition. No
more quick rising or hurrying about. Most everything took
an inordinate amount of energy and required deliberate
attention to bodily movement. A significant slowing of
inner movement occurred as well. Mom was content to do
less, be still longer, rest when needed. Life had been lived
as fully as possible.

Like the fox who gave himself to an unhurried, non-
fearful departure, so my mother gave herself to her
departure. I hope I can meet my death with such grace and
completeness. I hope I can resist clinging and clutching to
what has kept me here in this life. I'm definitely not there
yet, but each time I recall my mother's journey toward
aging and death I have greater strength to meet my own.

As I completed the last chapter of this memoir, I came
across a section in Pat Schneider's *How the Light Gets In* in

which she writes about her deceased mother. Each year Pat would visit her mother's gravesite and with each visit an animal of some sort would show up. One year a fox appeared. At that moment Pat realized it was time to let her mother go: "The fox was my mother, or a messenger from my mother, and the message was neither warm nor cold—neither blessing nor curse. It was rather, a farewell. I saw clearly that she was wild. She was beautiful. And she was on her own journey."[1]

I read those lines and, bingo, I was thrown back into a memory of fourteen years earlier. How could I have forgotten? Less than two weeks after Mom died, I traveled to Arkansas to attend a workshop. It was a wretched time for me. I felt bereft and could barely focus on being present. The second day of the workshop, in the early morning, I went for a walk in the nearby woods. Tears flowed as I plodded along miserably. All of a sudden I had this strange feeling I was not alone. I looked up to see a tattered, gray fox standing still on the hillside. Gazing. Gazing at me. Gazing and gazing. At that moment I had the strange sense, as Pat Schneider did, that the fox was either "my mother or a messenger from my mother." At the same time a doubting voice in me questioned why she would come as a fox, a ragged looking one at that. Now, these many years later, I believe the fox was sent that day to assure me of my mother's presence.

Coming across the two published pieces by Oliver and Schneider, and then recalling my own "fox experience," led me to wonder if my mother was making one more attempt to put my sorrow to rest. Finding Oliver's poem when I began the memoir and then Schneider's reflection as I completed it were two bookends opening and closing the lessons I wanted to share about my mother's life. Could the message be any clearer?

This sort of assurance from our deceased loved ones happens frequently. Sandra, a friend's mother said, "If I can send you a message, it will be with birds." After she died in the morning, her daughters went for a long walk and a hawk followed them all the way. Kathy Maxwell's mother asked Kathy to remember her whenever she saw a heart. What happened in the months to follow was phenomenal— hearts everywhere, even in the most unexpected places. After Tim Barry's dad died, he began finding pennies in strange places. Tim wrote, "I have come to believe, or at least hope, that means he is nearby. Often these pennies show up at important times, like one in front of our new home, and one when I was helping a handicapped lady from our church move late at night." My friend Carola spoke casually of a butterfly when we talked about her illness and aging. Three days after her sudden death, I sat at my computer and wept when I unexpectedly came across a video on the amazing metamorphosis of a butterfly.

The memory of seeing the fox after Mom's death brings me the greatest peace. It also confirms my sense of laying my sorrow to rest. In the past, almost every time I started to write about her, a keening heartache surfaced. So I formed a daily affirmation: "I am writing the memoir about Mom. I am willing to pay the price for it." The price, in large part, has been to allow the regrets and reality of her suffering to surface in my mind and heart. Just when I thought I'd cried the last tear, I came across another memory in my journal and up leapt more sadness. I've known for years the benefit of writing as a source of healing a sorrow but I most surely learned it all over again as I wrote this memoir.

It is much easier to hide or run from grief than to move toward it. Yet in the tending of what is stored in the heart there comes a gentle relief, an easing into a satisfied joy. Such has been my experience. As I conclude the story of my resilient mother, gratitude sings in my soul for the gift of this beloved woman in my life.

As if I still had not "gotten the message" about letting go of my mother and being at peace with her death, in the last months of editing this book, I came across Gordon Bok's song "Turning Toward the Morning."[2] No matter how I tried, I could not get that melody and the message out of my mind. Gordon Bok sings of the natural process of winter's darkness, of how the "old wind" sings of sorrow, and the heart grows lonely for the morning. But then Bok turns toward hope with the assurance that there is no need to be anxious or concerned, because winter darkness, wild wind, and sorrow are simply part of life. His hope lies in the seasons and the seas that keep rolling on, in the constancy of the world that keeps "turning toward the morning." I think now that this song is one last gift my mother brought to me.

Yes, Mom, like you, I will fly while I still have wings. I will draw forth courage from the example of your resiliency, gifted with hope that I, too, can keep turning toward the morning.

NOTES

1. THE BIRTH OF RESILIENCE

1. Francis Weller, *Entering the Healing Ground: Grief, Ritual and the Soul of the World* (Santa Rosa, CA: WisdomBridge Press, 2012).

2. FACING HARDSHIPS

1. Viktor Frankl, *Man's Search for Meaning* (Boston: Beacon Press, 2006).
2. Joan Chittister, *Scarred by Struggle, Transformed by Hope* (Grand Rapids, MI: Wm. B. Eerdmans Publishing Co., 2003).

4. THE BATHTUB QUESTION

1. Maya Angelou, *Even the Stars Look Lonesome* (New York: Bantam Books, 1998).
2. Rachel Naomi Remen, "Helping, Fixing, or Serving?," in *Daily Good: News That Inspires*, April 16, 2012, accessed September 13, 2014, http://www.dailygood.org/view.php?sid=218

5. FLY WHILE YOU STILL HAVE WINGS

1. Gail Godwin, *The Finishing School* (New York: Ballantine Books, 1999).
2. Trish Herbert, *Journeywell: A Guide to Quality Aging* (Edina, MN: Beaver's Pond Press, Inc., 2009).

3. Joan Chittister, *The Gift of Years: Growing Older Gracefully* (New York: Bluebridge, 2008).

6. A FIRM FOUNDATION OF FAITH

1. Emilie Griffin, *Souls in Full Sail: A Christian Spirituality for the Later Years* (Downers Grove, IL: Intervarsity Press, 2011).

7. THE BEST FRIEND I EVER HAD

1. Henry C. Simmons and Jane Wilson, *Soulful Aging: Ministry through the Stages of Adulthood* (Macon, GA: Smyth & Helwys Books, 2001).

2. Joan Chittister, *The Friendship of Women: A Spiritual Tradition* (New York: Sheed and Ward, 1999).

3. Mary Oliver, "The Gardener," *A Thousand Mornings: Poems* (New York: Penguin Books, 2012), 7–8.

8. WHEN A NEW DISABILITY ARRIVES

1. Jane R. Prétat, *Coming to Age: The Croning Years and Late-Life Transformation* (Toronto: Inner City Books, 1994).

2. Francis Weller, *Entering the Healing Ground: Grief, Ritual and the Soul of the World* (Santa Rosa, CA: WisdomBridge Press, 2012).

3. Florida Scott-Maxwell, *The Measure of My Days* (New York: Penguin Books, 1968).

4. Kathleen Dowling Singh, *The Grace in Dying: A Message of Hope, Comfort, and Spiritual Transformation* (New York: Harper Collins, 1998).

5. Jan Chozen Bays, *How to Train a Wild Elephant and Other Adventures in Mindfulness* (Boston: Shambhala Publications, Inc., 2011).

6. Simmons and Wilson, *Soulful Aging*.

9. CLIPPED WINGS

1. Mitch Albom, *Tuesdays with Morrie: An Old Man, a Young Man, and Life's Greatest Lesson* (New York: Doubleday, 1997).

10. THE GIFT OF THE SUN PORCH

1. Scott-Maxwell, *The Measure of My Days*.

2. Adyashanti, *Emptiness Dancing* (Boulder, CO: Sounds True, Inc., 2004).

3. Zora Neale Hurston, *Their Eyes Were Watching God* (Philadelphia: J. B. Lippincott Company, 1937).

4. Michael Himes, "The Suffering of Christ," in *Suffering and the Christian Life*, ed. Richard W. Miller (Maryknoll, NY: Orbis Books 2013), 113–125.

5. Jessica Powers, "If You Have Nothing," in *The Selected Poetry of Jessica Powers*, eds. Regina Siegfried and Robert Morneau (Washington, DC: ICS Publications, 1999), 91.

6. May Sarton, *At Seventy: A Journal* (New York: W.W. Norton and Co. Inc., 1984).

7. Joyce Hutchison and Joyce Rupp, *May I Walk You Home?: Courage and Comfort for Caregivers of the Very Ill* (Notre Dame, IN: Ave Maria Press, 2009).

8. Rabindranath Tagore, "The Last Word," in *The Heart of God: Prayers of Rabindranath Tagore* (Boston: Tuttle Publishing, 1997).

11. A BOOK OF REGRETS

1. Eben Alexander, *Proof of Heaven: A Neurosurgeon's Journey into the Afterlife* (New York: Simon and Schuster, 2012).

2. Weller, *Entering the Healing Ground*.

EPILOGUE: TURNING TOWARD THE MORNING

1. Pat Schneider, *How the Light Gets In: Writing as a Spiritual Practice* (New York: Oxford University Press, 2013), 218.

2. Gordon Bok, Ann Mayo Muir, and Ed Trickett, "Turning Toward the Morning," in *Turning Toward the Morning*, 1975, Folk-Legacy Records, Inc., compact disc.

READER'S GUIDE

1. THE BIRTH OF RESILIENCE

1. The author refers to resilience as a "quality of inner strength." How would you describe what resilience means to you? In what ways have you come to know this quality in your life? How might this quality generate courage and confidence when you face difficulties?

Among other gifts, Hilda Rupp inherited resiliency from her ancestral aunts. What gifts of your ancestral lineage have you inherited? How do these gifts serve to guide the way you live?

2. What is "ancestral grief"? How did it enable the author to enter her healing process? Looking back into your own heritage, what sorrows have been passed on to you? Has grief from the past influenced your life in some way? How might an awareness of "ancestral grief" be of benefit to you or those whom you counsel or assist with personal growth issues?

Who are your mentors of strength and courage? Describe one of them. How has he or she touched your life?

3. Take some time to reflect on the central values or qualities that give your life meaning and purpose. Summarize these in a short statement.

4. What did you find most helpful in this chapter? What leaves you with questions yet to be answered? What would you want to add to the author's insights?

2. FACING HARDSHIPS

1. "Inconveniences and privations abounded." What were some of the significant hardships that Hilda experienced? How did she cope with

them? What modern-day hardships parallel those she experienced? How might Hilda's attitude influence the way these persons or groups respond to their adversities?

2. The author poses this question: "How do we continue to keep the flame of hope alive in a corner of our heart when hardship strains to snuff it out?" What is your response?

3. Viktor Frankl believed that we have the ability to choose our attitude and response to the harsh realities of life. What is your opinion about this belief? When have you had to choose a response in a difficult time? What was this response like? Did this response help or hinder you?

4. How did an appreciation of the natural world benefit Hilda in her later years? Has an awareness of creation's beauty affected your experience of life when it is not going well? If so, how? What most helps you to get through difficult times?

5. "Even a small kindness makes a difference." Pause to reflect on the small kindnesses that have made a difference in your life. Which ones have meant the most to you?

6. What did you find most helpful in this chapter? What leaves you with questions yet to be answered? What would you want to add to the author's insights?

3. THE SHADOW SIDE

1. "Our best qualities have a shadow side to them." How would you describe what the psychological "shadow" is? Recall a time when you became aware of the shadow side of one of your best qualities. What prompted this awareness? What happened after you discovered it?

2. How did Lester's verbal abuse affect Hilda's belief in herself? How might she have responded differently? In what ways do other kinds of abuse affect those who are abused? The author asked her mother to write ten good things about herself. Are there other ways that self-esteem might be nurtured?

3. A cultural acceptance of patriarchy contributed to Lester's abusive behavior. What else influenced the way he treated Hilda? What socially acceptable behaviors today contribute to a sense of unworthiness or powerlessness in others?

4. Hilda found it difficult to be compassionate and kind to herself when she was hurting. How do you extend comfort and kindness to yourself when you experience hurt?

5. Pause to reflect on your personal heritage. Make a list with two columns. Under the first column, list the positive qualities and characteristics of your heritage. Under the second column, list the drawbacks and hindrances you've inherited. Which of them seem to predominate in your life?

6. What did you find most helpful in this chapter? What leaves you with questions yet to be answered? What would you want to add to the author's insights?

4. THE BATHTUB QUESTION

1. How did the question about the bathtub affect the author? How did the question serve to benefit her? Have you ever been asked a question that catapulted you into a part of your life that needed attention? If so, how did this happen and how did you respond to it?

2. The author acknowledges: "I've unknowingly spoken with condescension or acted in a demeaning manner toward people in their later years." What are some of the ways she did this? Have you ever heard others speak this way? What attitudinal or behavioral changes need to occur in order to lessen this approach to older people?

3. What are some key insights the author learned about her mother's aging? What is your view of your own aging process? How do you hope to experience your elderhood? What would be most helpful for you? What would be least helpful? If you were asked to describe yourself as an older person, what would you want the description to include?

4. Have you ever found yourself in a situation like the author's, in which you ended up trying to help someone and stepped beyond the boundaries

of what was needed? Has someone done this to you? If so, what did it feel like? What would you have preferred to happen?

5. How would you respond to these questions the author raises: "How much do we protect older people by guarding them from certain foods, or moving them from their homes so they don't leave the stove burners on, or take their car keys away so they avoid an accident? When do we begin lending our voice regarding their medical procedures?"

6. What did you find most helpful in this chapter? What leaves you with questions yet to be answered? What would you want to add to the author's insights?

5. FLY WHILE YOU STILL HAVE WINGS

1. Reflect on some older people you have known who manifested a zest for life. How did they do this? Which of their approaches to life are ones you would like to emulate in your own life?

2. Review what Gail Godwin suggests about not "congealing" and Joan Chittister's two approaches to aging. How did Godwin describe the two types of people "walking around on this earth?" What terms does Chittister use? Do you have other images you would use? What did Hilda do to remain fluid and flexible in spirit?

3. Hilda's sense of humor aided her as she aged. What were some ways in which this occurred? What part does a sense of humor have in your life? Give an example of when humor eased a difficult situation you were in.

4. The author became a closer friend to her mother through their travels together. Are there some life events and experiences that have brought you closer to those you love and appreciate? Recall some specific instances.

5. Hilda's advice to Joyce about growing older was to "go with the flow." What do you think of this response? If you were asked to give advice or a suggestion about growing older, what would you offer?

6. What did you find most helpful in this chapter? What leaves you with questions yet to be answered? What would you want to add to the author's insights?

6. A FIRM FOUNDATION OF FAITH

1. "Little do we know when we are young what might sustain us as we grow old." What were some ways that Hilda's faith influenced her life? How did this faith sustain her as she grew older?

2. The author chose not to ask Hilda about her personal experience of God. Do you agree with this decision? Why or why not? How might a conversation with Hilda about this topic have made a difference in the mother-daughter relationship?

3. "Organized religion naturally existed as part of her personal journey. . . ." What has your experience been regarding organized religion? In what ways has it affected or not affected your life? Do you envision participation in an organized religion as being of benefit in your later years? If yes, what might these benefits be for you?

4. "As Mom grew older, I kept hearing new things from her in regard to her personal faith and religious beliefs." What were some of these changes that the author noticed? What have you observed about changes or modifications of your own, or others whom you know, in regard to personal faith beliefs and spiritual practices?

5. Read the quote by Emilie Griffin that opens this chapter. Would you agree with Griffin that the structure of faith is the best thing one can build for the future? Is there anything you would insert that is more vital than the structure of faith?

6. What did you find most helpful in this chapter? What leaves you with questions yet to be answered? What would you want to add to the author's insights?

7. THE BEST FRIEND I EVER HAD

1. What led to Hilda's discovering her best friend late in life? How would you describe the friendship that evolved between Hilda and Wilda? What aspects of this friendship most resonate with you?

2. Wilda awakened "innate inclinations" in the author's mother. What were some of these inclinations and how did they affect Hilda's aging? Do

you have a sense of some of your own unlived inclinations and, if so, what are they? What might you do to allow them to be birthed?

3. The author writes about her mother's loneliness. How did this loneliness reveal itself? What have you observed about older people and loneliness? How do you cope with loneliness when it arises in you?

4. How did Wilda's death affect Hilda? How did she respond to this death? What do you think about the author's comment on Hilda's grief being "the inevitable consequence of out-living the significant persons in one's life?" How do you currently cope with grief?

5. Reflect on friendships you have known. Which ones have been most surprising? Most rewarding? What have you gleaned from these friendships? What do you believe to be some of the essential qualities of a beneficial friendship?

6. What did you find most helpful in this chapter? What leaves you with questions yet to be answered? What would you want to add to the author's insights?

8. WHEN A NEW DISABILITY ARRIVES

1. The author writes, "Every new biological limitation challenged my mother's resiliency." What were Hilda's developing physical limitations? How did they affect her resiliency?

2. Hilda entered into a period of depression after having a heart attack. How did she and the author respond to this mental and emotional change? What would you suggest to someone older who experiences depression?

3. Is there a way that one can prepare for increasing disability of body, mind, or spirit? Are you currently sensing your own increasing physical frailty, or do you know someone who is? What has it been like for you, or for that person? What approach or action could alleviate, or lessen, the inherent struggles that often ensue due to the developing physical infirmities associated with aging?

4. Give some reasons why an older person might hide or avoid talking about increasing disability. Have you known anyone who has done this?

Have you experienced someone speaking incessantly about their physical health issues? How do you acknowledge your own changing physical condition?

5. "Sometimes a gift lies hidden in what we resist or resent." What gift lay hidden in Hilda's depression? Have you received a gift after going through a difficult or unwanted experience? If so, describe this gift.

6. What did you find most helpful in this chapter? What leaves you with questions yet to be answered? What would you want to add to the author's insights?

9. CLIPPED WINGS

1. The chapter begins with this statement from the author: "What serves as inner strength during one period of life can become a liability in another." How did this happen for Hilda? When has a strength of yours become a liability?

2. Hilda found the move from independence to dependence a challenging one. What was most difficult about this transition for her? How have you known independence and dependence? Is there an aspect of being dependent that you find to be especially hard to accept? What might one do to be more accepting of a dependent mode of living?

3. "Vulnerability and humility accompany dependency." As you reflect on this insight, recall times when you felt a certain vulnerability. What led to your feeling vulnerable? How did you respond to this? Is there a way that some of the uncomfortableness might have been lessened?

4. The author writes of the need for older persons to have an advocate regarding their medical issues. What are some specific ways that a supportive presence might be of help to those in elderhood when they go for medical treatment or diagnosis? Have you been an advocate for someone older, or have you been the recipient of this kind of support?

5. Hilda found ways to continue to give to others during the time when she faced increasing dependency. What were some of these gestures? Are there other ways you have observed, either in yourself or another, that

allow for being able to contribute to the benefit of others even while being in a "receiving mode"?

6. What did you find most helpful in this chapter? What leaves you with questions yet to be answered? What would you want to add to the author's insights?

10. THE GIFT OF THE SUN PORCH

1. What was the gift of the sun porch? How did it come to Hilda? What effect did it have on her remaining years?

2. What are some of the ways that the author denied her mother's impending death? What kept her from the truth of this reality? How might the author have responded differently? What do you observe in society's approach to death? Do you notice denial or acceptance, or something other than that? What might the reasons for this approach be?

3. What do you think of Hilda taking care of her own funeral arrangements? How comfortable are you in discussing end-of-life preparations, either your own or those of a loved one? Are there some topics you hesitate to bring into the conversation? What are some specific things you can do to prepare for your death? Have you taken care of any of them? If not, what holds you back?

4. What was Hilda's "Gethsemane?" What part did this experience have in her gradual acceptance of physical diminishment and her future death?

5. Read Jessica Powers' poem "If You Have Nothing." Discuss the relationship between this poem and Hilda's time on the sun porch. If Hilda had expressed why she liked the poem so much, what might she have said?

6. What did you find most helpful in this chapter? What leaves you with questions yet to be answered? What would you want to add to the author's insights?

11. A BOOK OF REGRETS

1. How would you describe what regret is?

2. How did the author experience regret in regard to her relationship with her mother? What are some of the specific things the author wished she had, or had not, done? What effect did regret have on her mental and emotional state?

3. Look back on your life. Do you find some regrets there? If so, what are they, and how have you dealt with them?

4. The author chose honesty in responding to her mother's concern about the possibility of having to live in a nursing home. Would you have spoken differently to Hilda about this concern?

5. The author reflects on an insight of Francis Weller's: "There comes a time in grieving when we have to stop dragging our bag of regrets around and lay them aside." How did she lay her bag of remorse aside and eventually move on?

6. What did you find most helpful in this chapter? What leaves you with questions yet to be answered? What would you want to add to the author's insights?

AVE

AVE MARIA PRESS

Founded in 1865, Ave Maria Press,
a ministry of the Congregation of
Holy Cross, is a Catholic publishing
company that serves the spiritual and
formative needs of the Church and its
schools, institutions, and ministers;
Christian individuals and families; and
others seeking spiritual nourishment.

For a complete listing of titles from

Ave Maria Press

Sorin Books

Forest of Peace

Christian Classics

visit www.avemariapress.com

AVE MARIA PRESS
Notre Dame, IN
A Ministry of the United States Province of Holy Cross